THE CUTE & SIMPLE DRAWING BOOK FOR TEENS

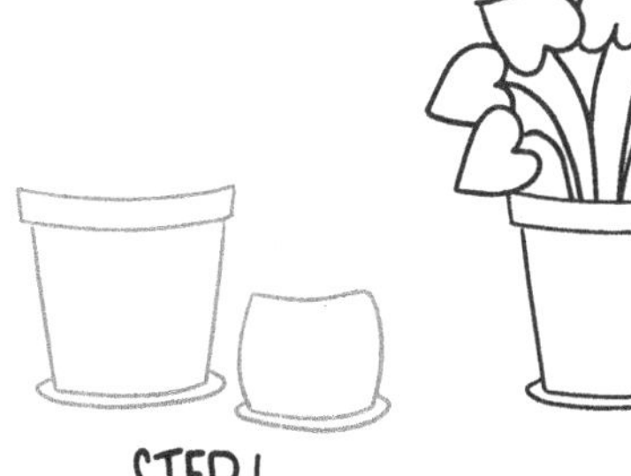

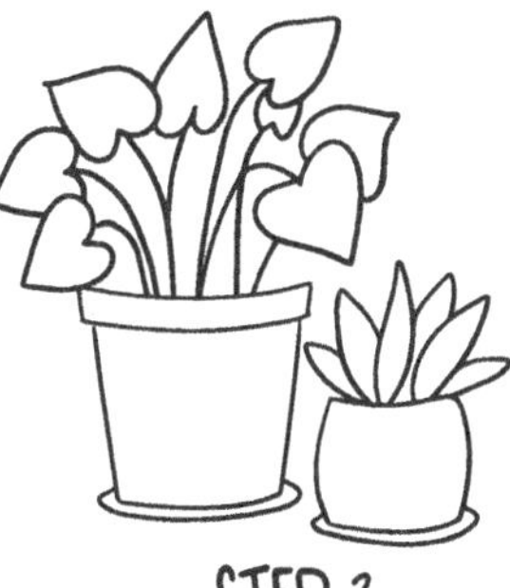

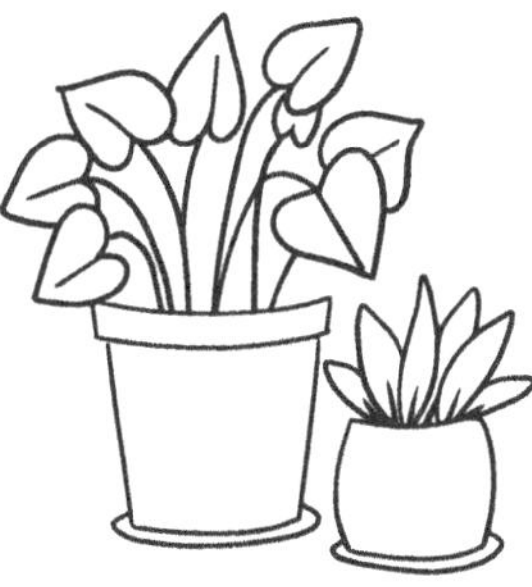

EMAIL US AT

prettysimplebooks@gmail.com

TO GET FREE GOODIES!

Just title the email "Drawing for Teens"
And we will send some extra surprises your way!

The Cute and Simple Drawing Book for Teens

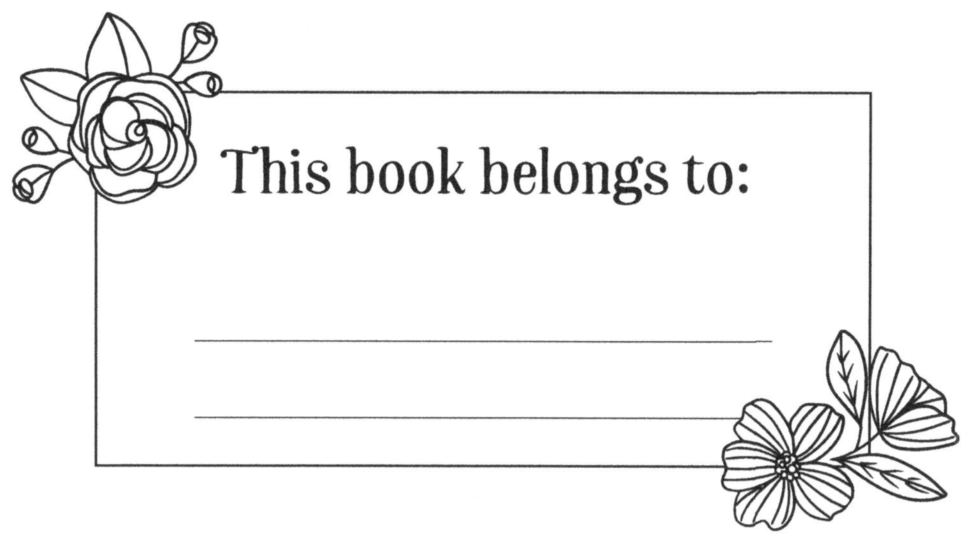
This book belongs to:

hey there!

We're so glad you picked up this book! Whether you're looking to improve your sketching skills or just hoping for a fun way to pass the time, this book will serve you well! We put together 48 simple and fun illustrations and broken down a how-to in 4 easy steps. Read each step with the corresponding drawing and then try it on your own! 5 minutes later you're on your way to the next drawing. You made it here... all that's left to do is grab your pencil or favorite pen and turn the page!

If you enjoy the book, feel free to check out some of the other books from Pretty Simple Press and email us at prettysimplepress@gmail.com for any questions or concerns and we will be happy to get back with you!

let's draw!

contents

Stack of Books....pg. 6
Pumpkin....pg. 8
Roller Skate....pg. 10
Fall Leaves....pg. 12
Sushi....pg. 14
Peace Sign....pg. 16
Vintage Telephone....pg. 18
Donut....pg. 20
Picnic Basket....pg. 22
Suitcases....pg. 24
Vintage Camera....pg. 26
Teapot....pg. 28
Owl....pg. 30
House....pg. 32
Bicycle....pg. 34
Mushroom....pg. 36
Happy Sunshine....pg. 38
Acorn....pg. 40
Daisy....pg. 42
French Fries....pg. 44
Snowflake....pg. 46
Cake....pg. 48
Chicken....pg. 50
Flamingo....pg. 52
Honey Bee....pg. 54
Lemons....pg. 56
Lemonade....pg. 58
Cute Storefront....pg. 60
Cactus....pg. 62
Ice Cream....pg. 64
Mixer....pg. 66
Strawberries....pg. 68
Mermaid....pg. 70
Swan....pg. 72
Swimsuits....pg. 74
Unicorn....pg. 76
Poppies....pg. 78
Succulents....pg. 80
Tulip....pg. 82
Cup of Tea....pg. 84
Sunflower....pg. 86
Flower Bouquet....pg. 88
House Plants....pg. 90
Cupcake....pg. 92
Rose....pg. 94
Typewriter....pg. 96
Beehive....pg. 98
Butterfly....pg. 100

Let's draw a

stack of books

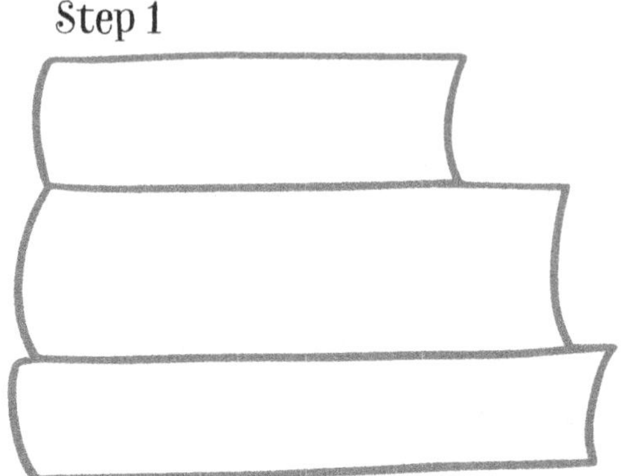

1. With a pencil draw a stack of rectangles making curved lines on the right side.

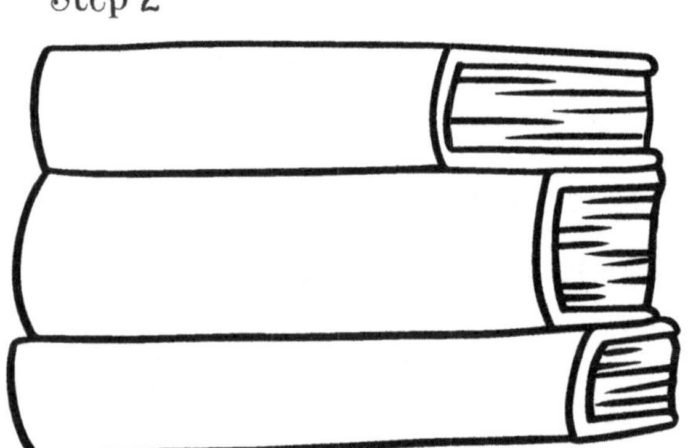

2. With a drawing pen trace over your pencil drawing. Add spines and pages of the books to the right side of the rectangles to form a stack of books.

3. With a pen add details to the spines of each book.

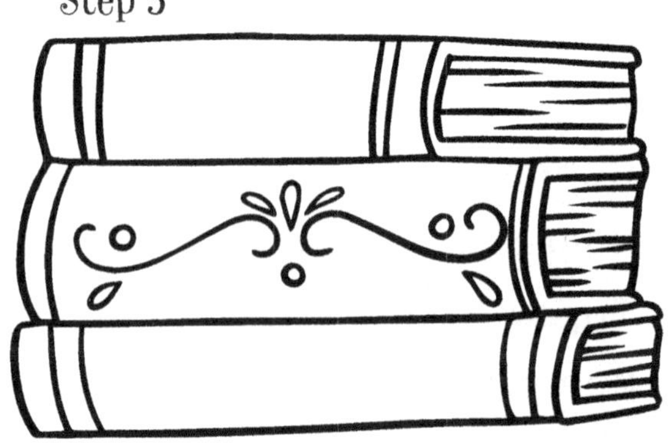

4. Finish the stack of books by drawing a little tea cup on the top.

Step 4

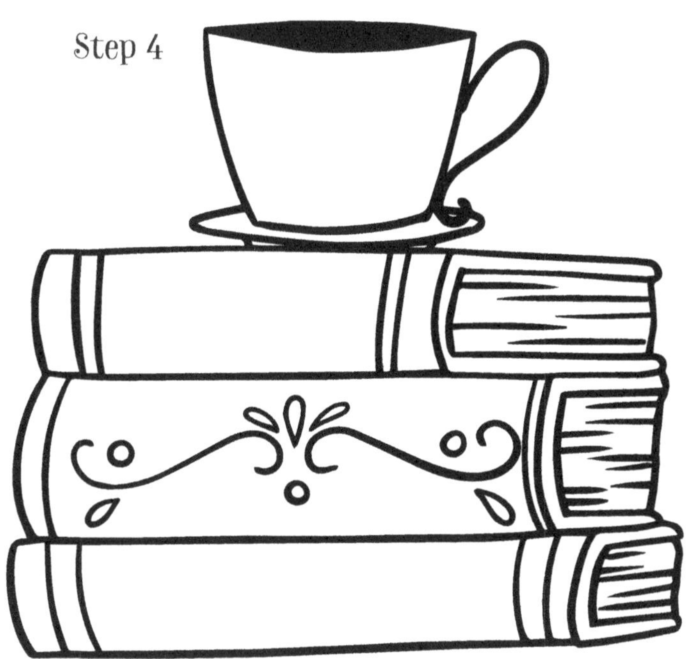

Draw your stack of books below:

Let's draw a

pumpkin

Step 1

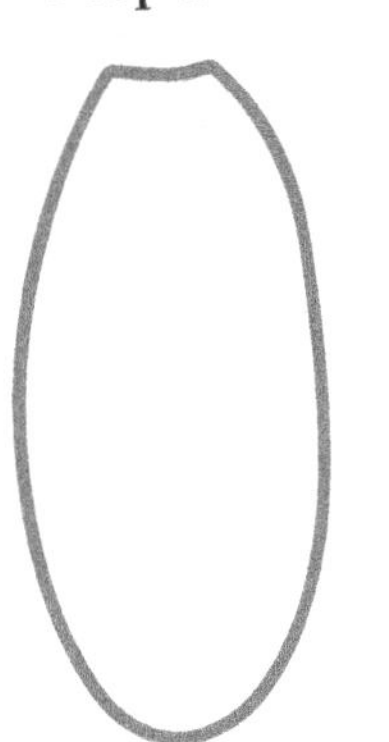

1. With a pencil draw an oval.

Step 2

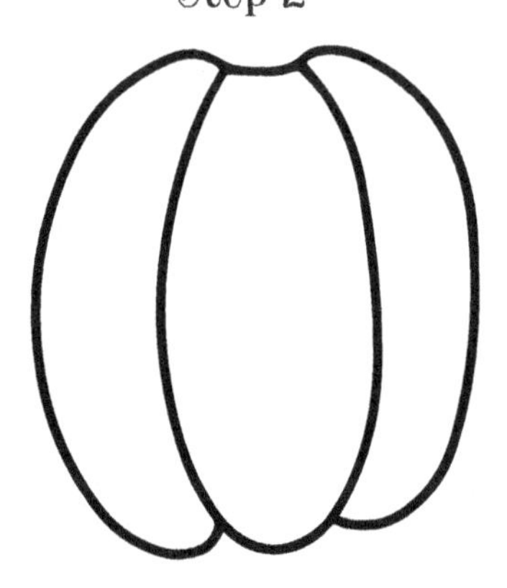

2. With a drawing pen trace over your pencil drawing. Add a half ovals on each side.

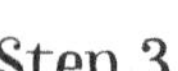

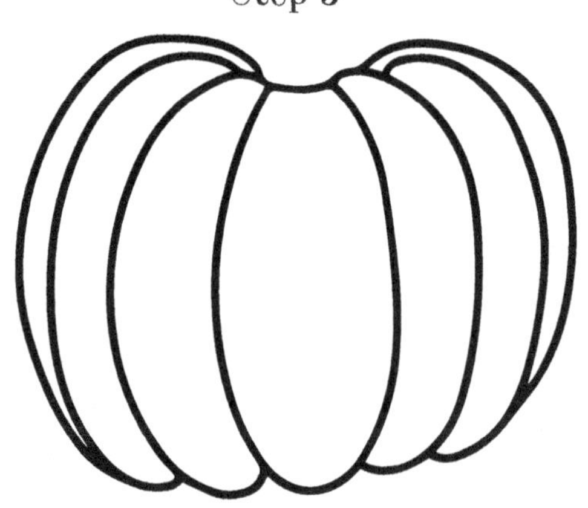

3. With a pen continue to add thinner half ovals on each side to form a pumpkin.

4. Finish the drawing by adding a stem at the top of the pumpkin.

Step 4

Draw your pumpkin below:

Let's draw a

roller skate

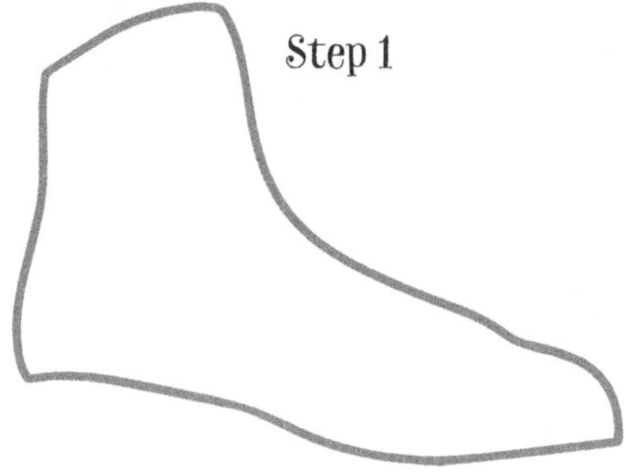

1. With a pencil draw a boot shaped object.

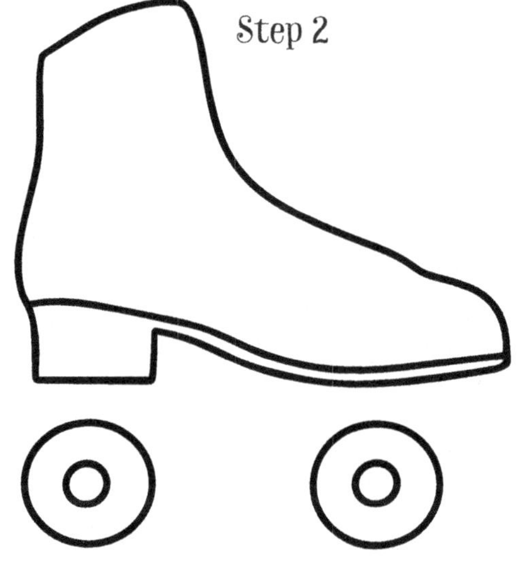

2. With a drawing pen trace over your pencil drawing. Add the heal and bottom portion of the skate. Leaving some space below, draw the wheels of the skate.

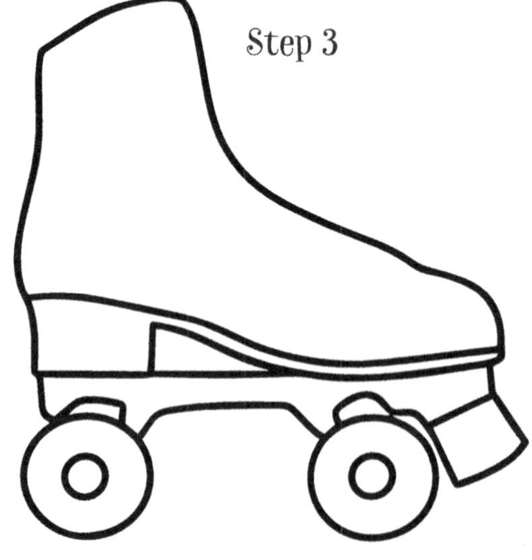

3. With a pen connect the bottom of the skate to the wheels. Add the skate stopper at the toe portion.

4. Finish the skate by adding holes and a shoe string. Draw accent dotted seams.

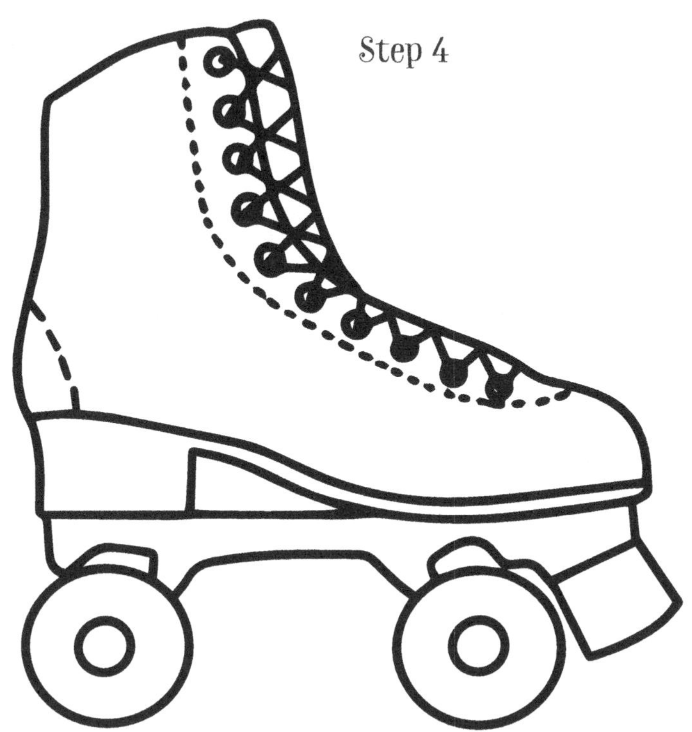

Draw your roller skate below:

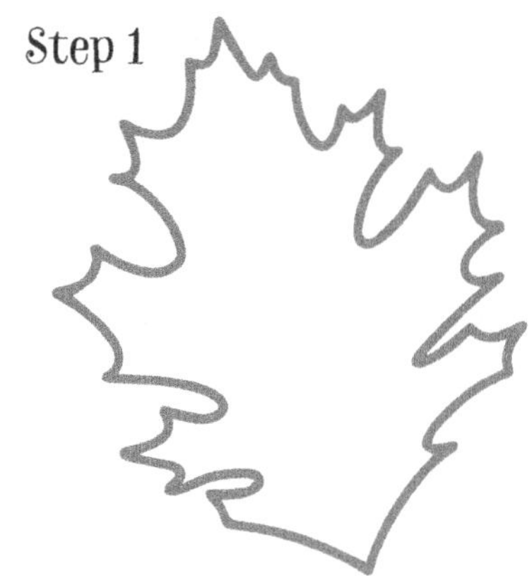

Let's draw

Fall leaves

1. With a pencil draw a leaf.

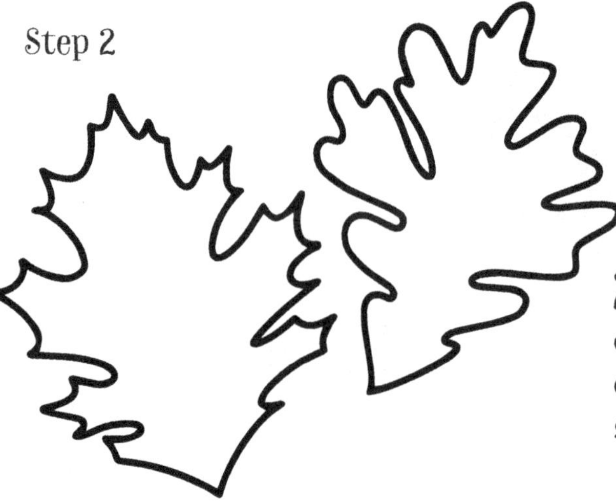

2. With a drawing pen trace over your pencil drawing. Draw a second leaf of a different style.

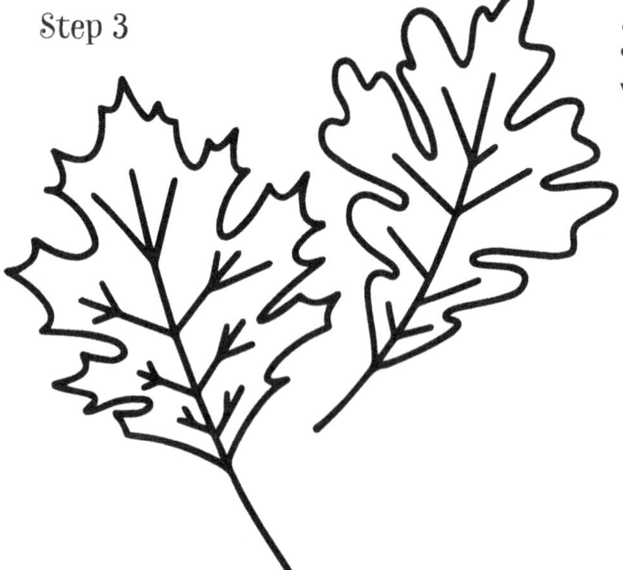

3. With a pen add stems and veins to each leaf.

4. Finish the drawing by adding smaller accent leaves.

Step 4

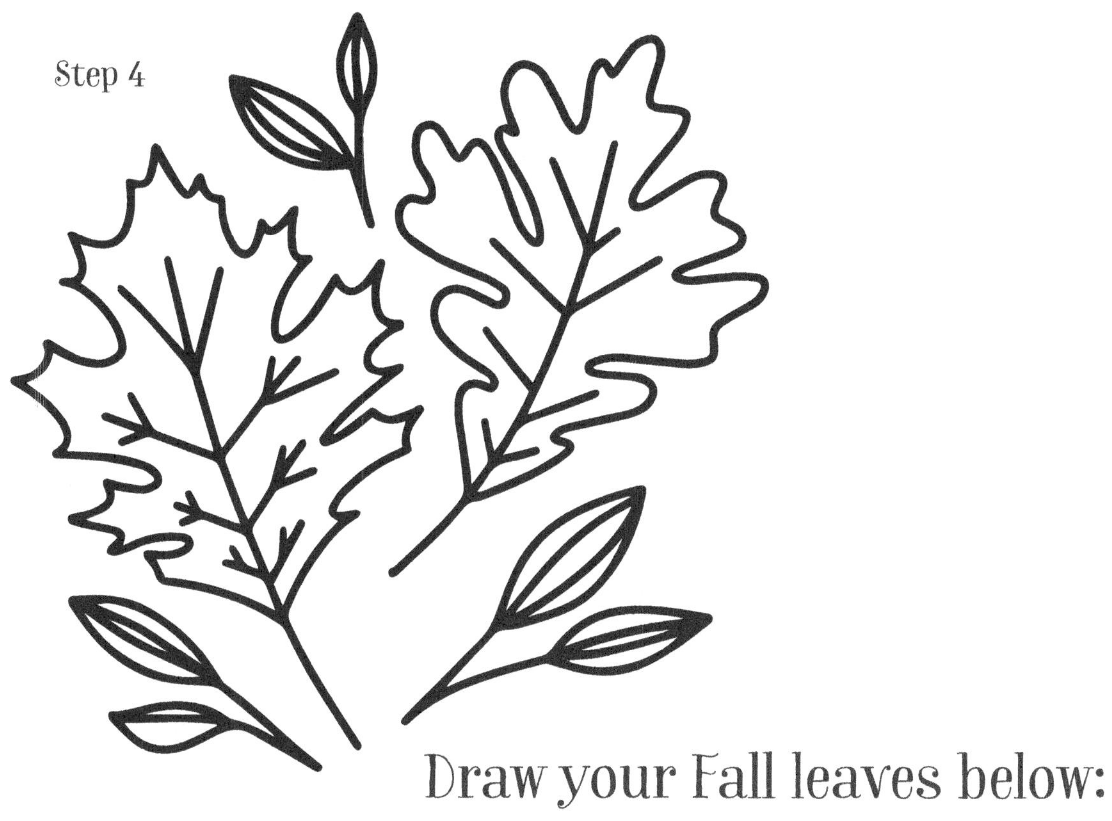

Draw your Fall leaves below:

Let's draw

sushi

Step 1

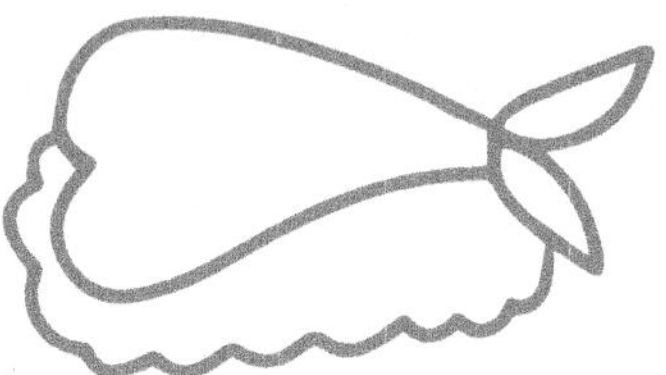

1. With a pencil draw a shrimp on a rectangle of sushi rice to create shrimp nigiri.

Step 2

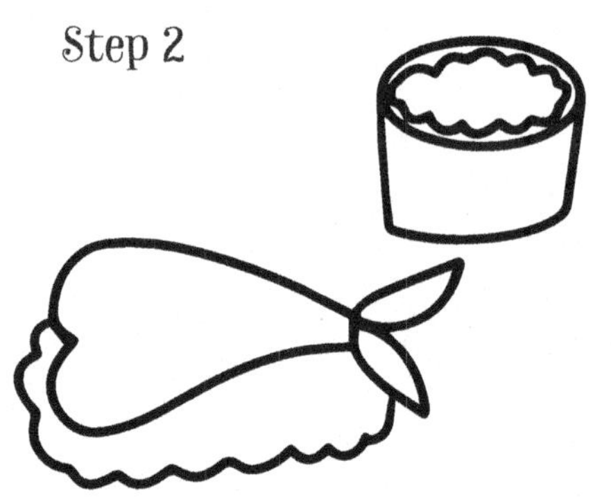

2. With a drawing pen trace over your pencil drawing. Draw a short cylinder with rice in the center to create maki.

Step 3

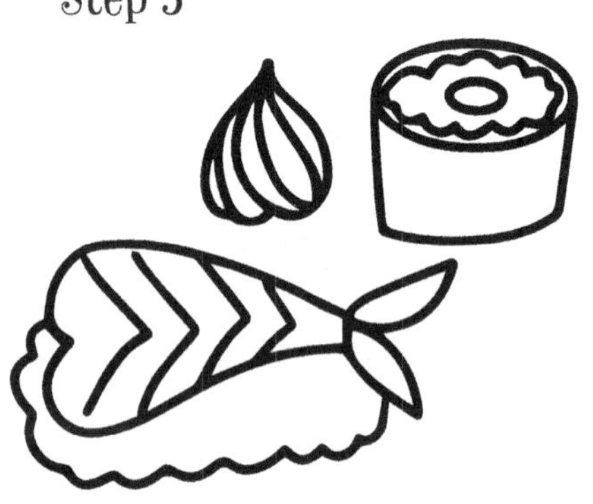

3. With a pen add accent lines on the shrimp. Draw a portion of wasabi and a circle in the center of the maki.

4. Finish the drawing by adding a set of chopsticks.

Step 4

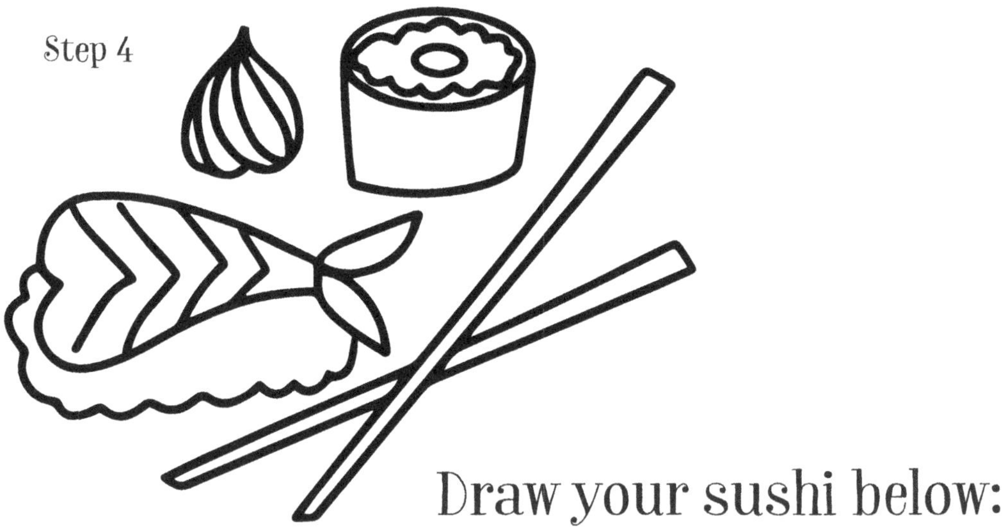

Draw your sushi below:

Let's draw a

peace sign

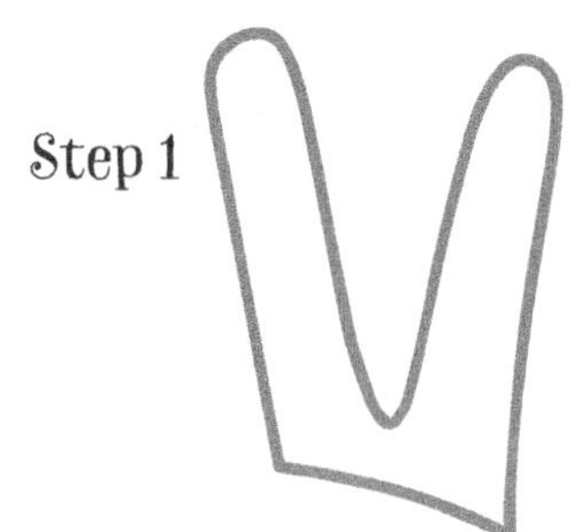

1. With a pencil draw a pointer and middle finger forming a "v".

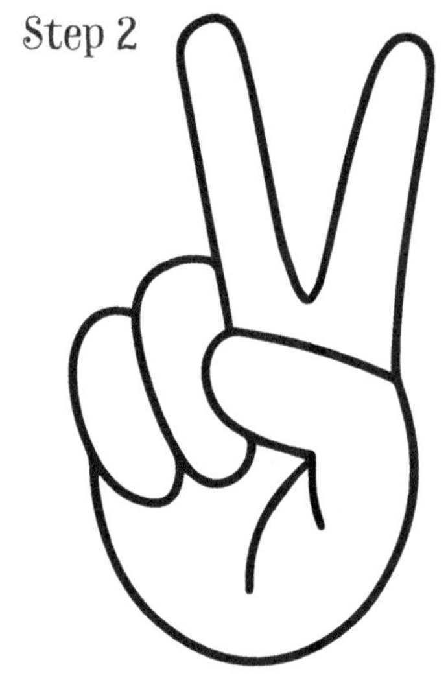

2. With a drawing pen trace over your pencil drawing. Draw a half circle and remaining fingers bent together.

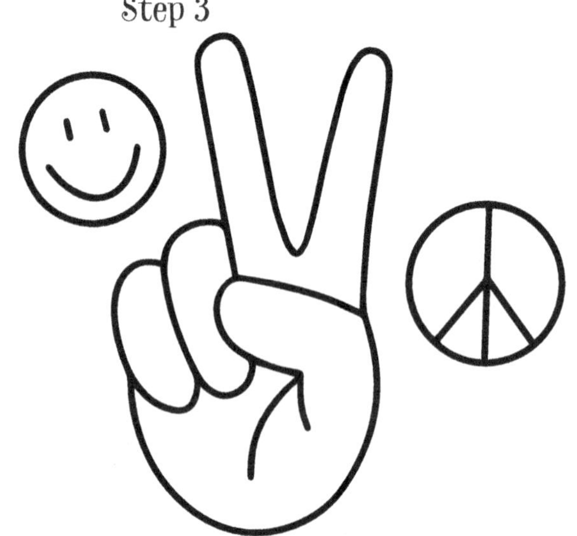

3. With a pen add two circles. Add in a smiley face to one circle and lines to form a peace sign in the second circle.

4. Finish the drawing by adding little accent flowers and the word "peace" curved around the bottom portion of the hand.

Step 4

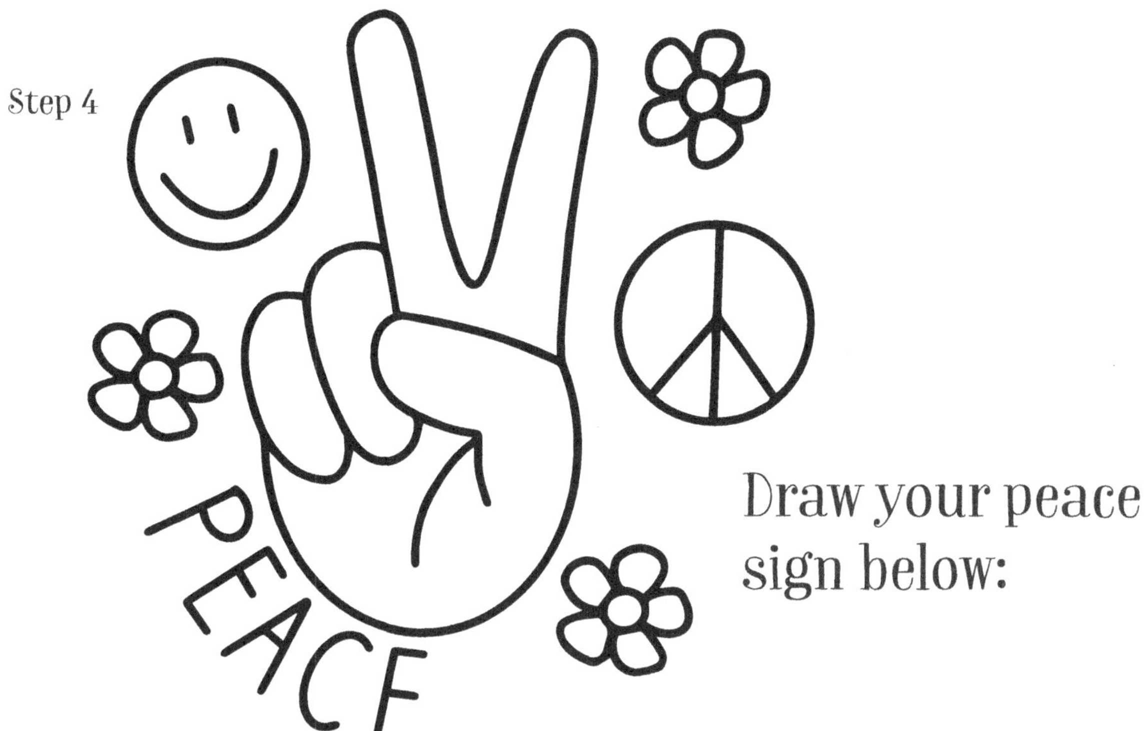

Draw your peace sign below:

Let's draw a

vintage telephone

Step 1

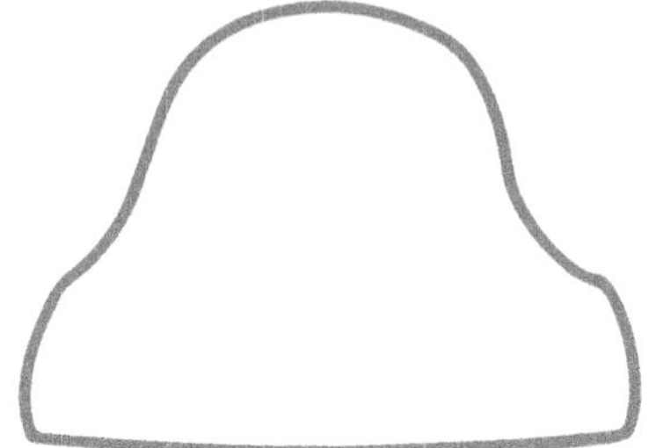

1. With a pencil draw a bell shape to create the base of the telephone.

Step 2

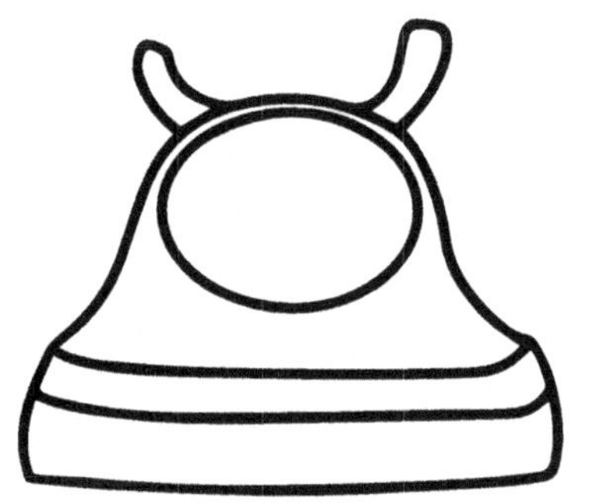

2. With a drawing pen trace over your pencil drawing. Draw a circle at the top of the bell shape. Draw two lines at the bottom of the bell shape. Add two hook shapes at the top of the telephone to form the handset rest.

3. With a pen add a second circle in the first circle to form the phone dial. Draw the phone handset on top of the two hook shapes.

Step 3

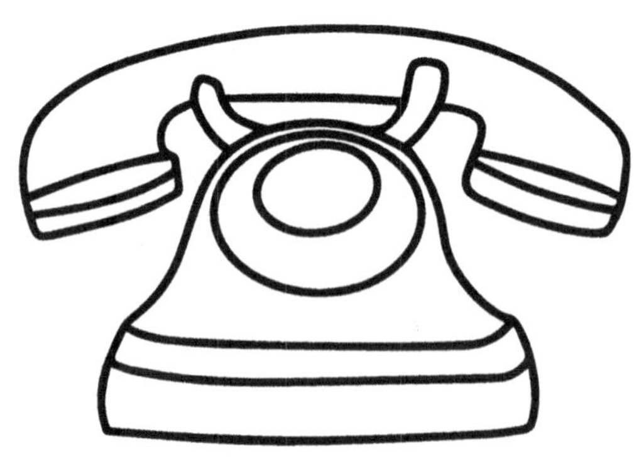

4. Finish the drawing by adding a curly cord connecting the handset to the base of the phone. Add smaller circles for the dial numbers.

Step 4

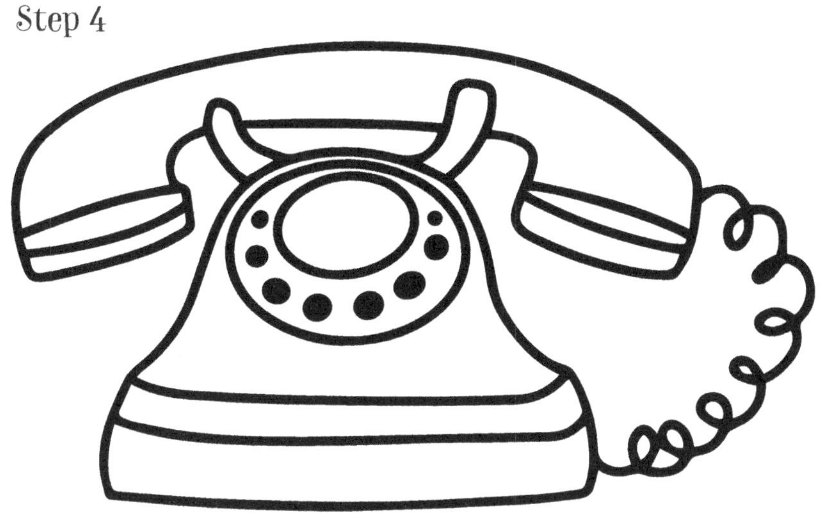

Draw your vintage telephone below:

Let's draw a
donut

Step 1

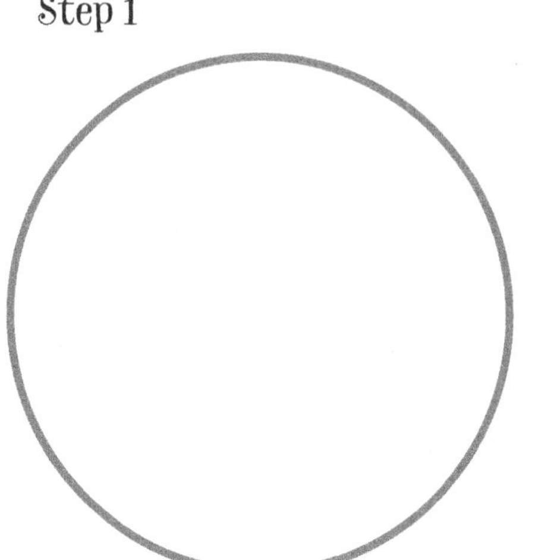

1. With a pencil draw a circle.

Step 2

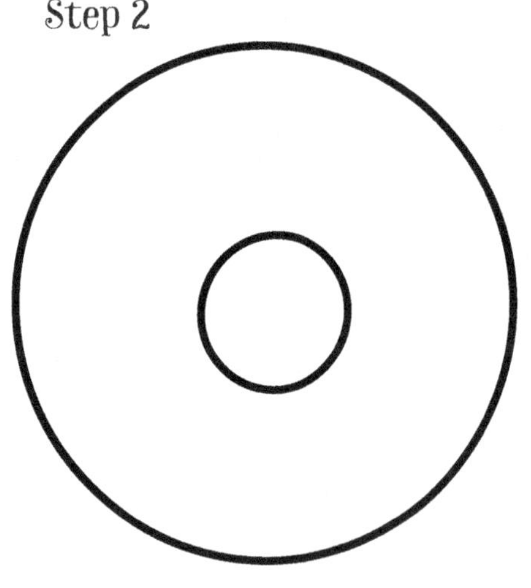

2. With a drawing pen trace over your pencil drawing. Draw a circle in the center of the circle to form a donut.

3. With a pen add a wavy design around the inside edge of the donut to create icing.

Step 3

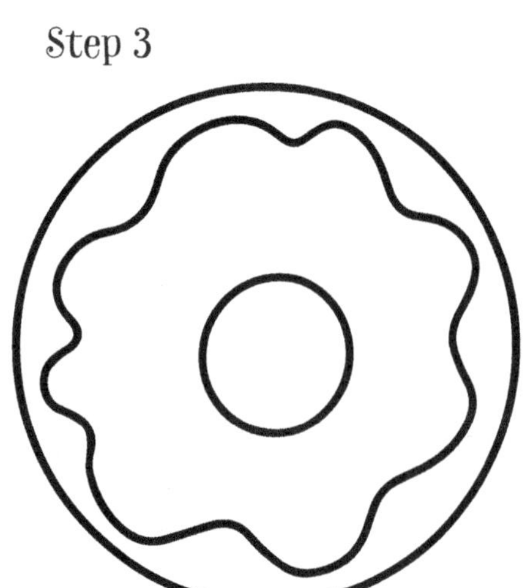

4. Finish the drawing by adding sprinkles all over the donut icing.

Step 4

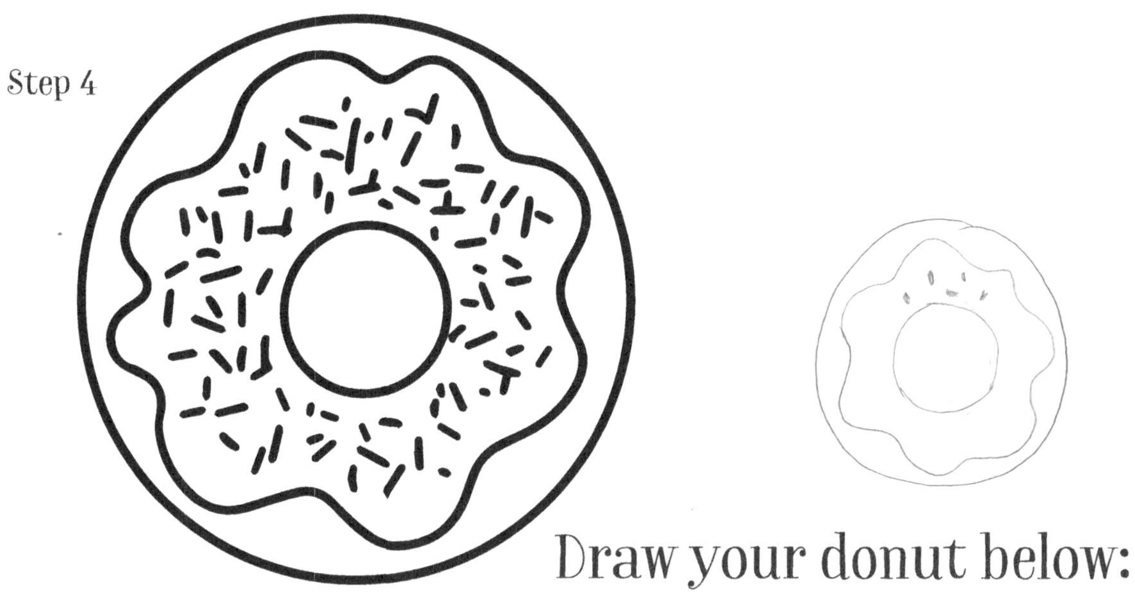

Draw your donut below:

Let's draw a
picnic basket

Step 1

1. With a pencil draw a trapezoid shape.

Step 2

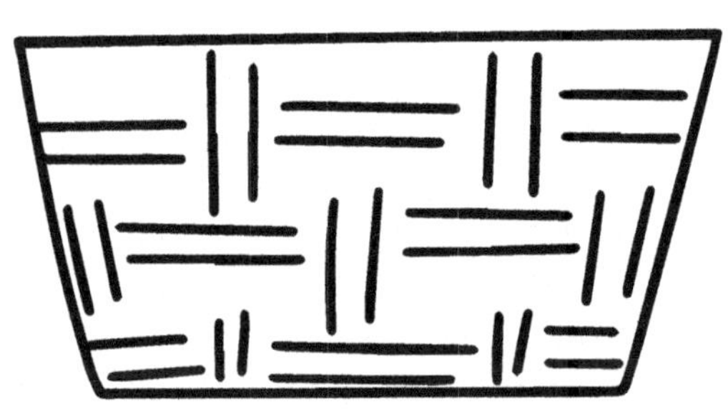

2. With a drawing pen trace over your pencil drawing. Draw varying pairs of vertical and horizontal lines to create a picnic basket.

3. With a pen add a handle and a lid to the top side of the picnic basket.

Step 3

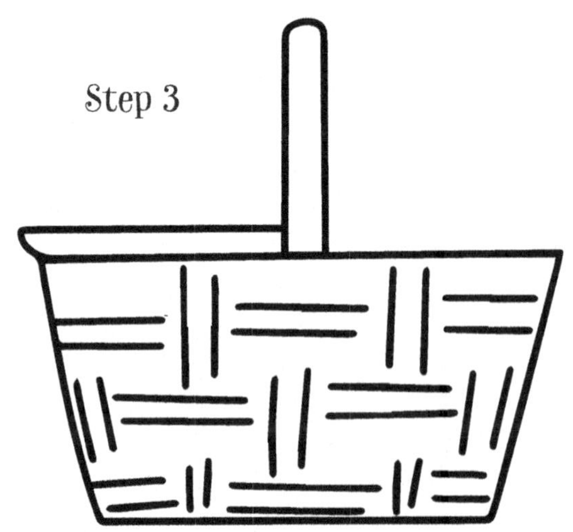

4. Finish the drawing by adding a thermos and loaf of bread coming out of the right side of the picnic basket. Add blanket at the bottom of the basket.

Step 4

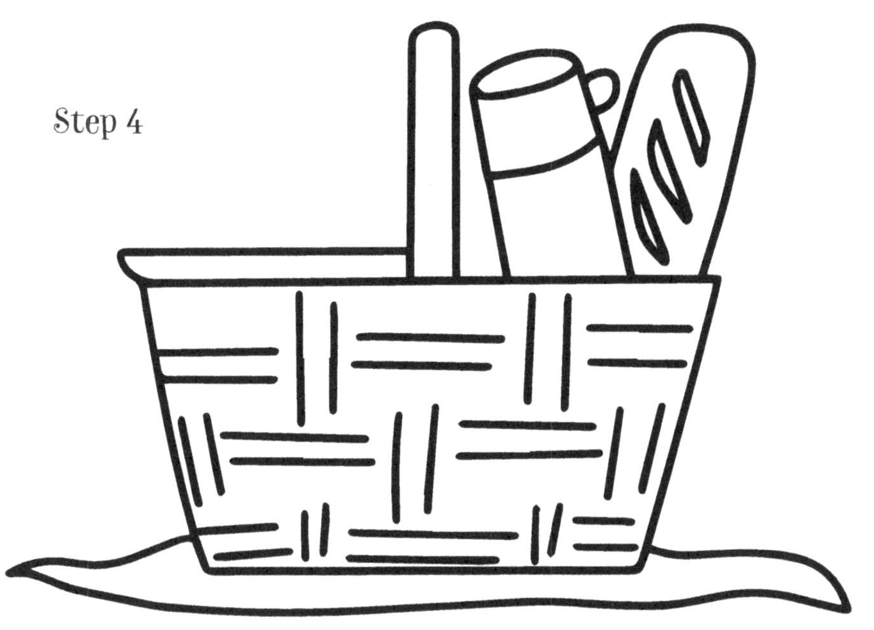

Draw your picnic basket below:

Let's draw suitcases

Step 1

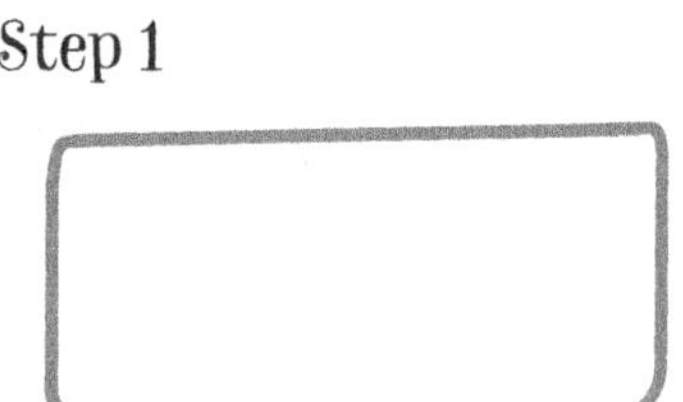

1. With a pencil draw a rectangle.

Step 2

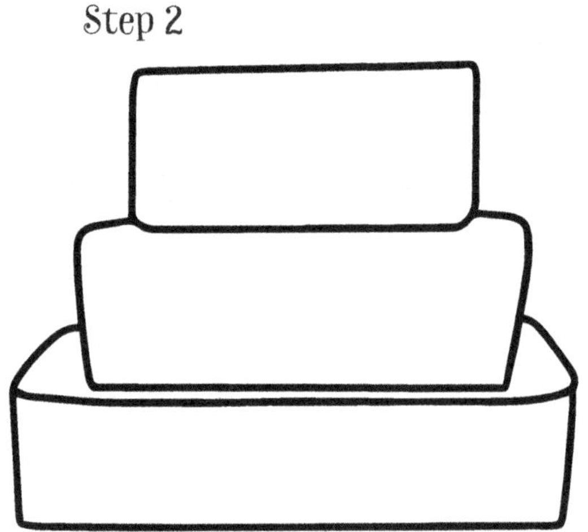

2. With a drawing pen trace over your pencil drawing. Draw a larger rectangle under the first, then draw a third larger rectangle to form a stack of suitcases.

3. With a pen add lines to the center of each rectangle to create the suitcase openings.

Step 3

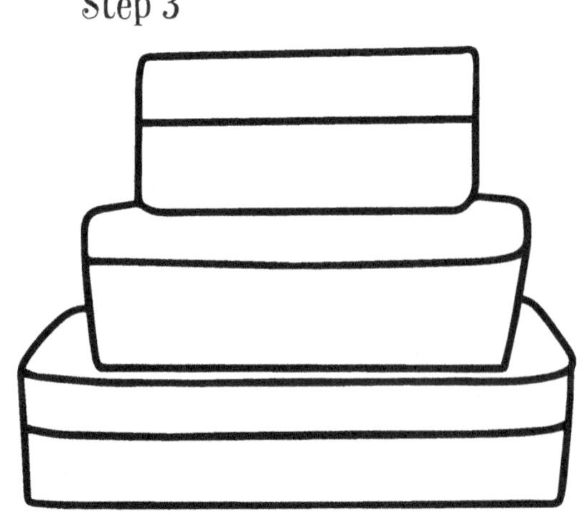

4. Finish the drawing by adding handles and clasps to each suitcase.

Step 4

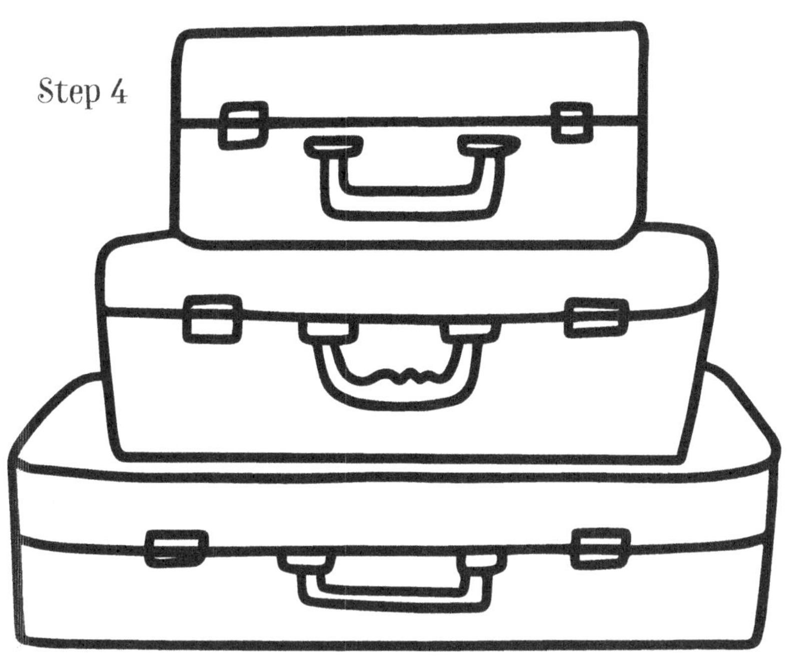

Draw your suitcases below:

Let's draw a
vintage camera

Step 1

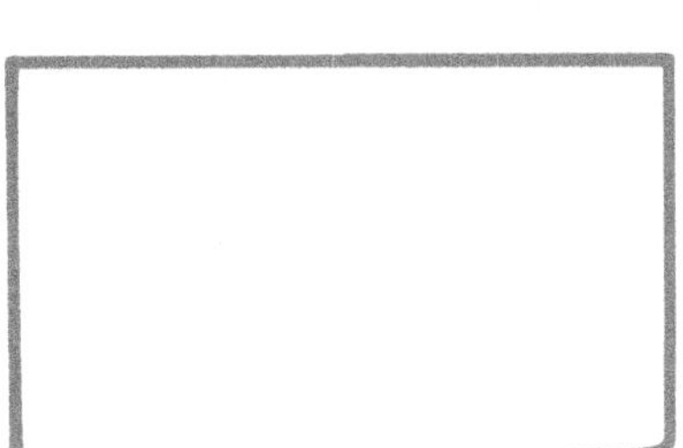

1. With a pencil draw a rectangle.

Step 2

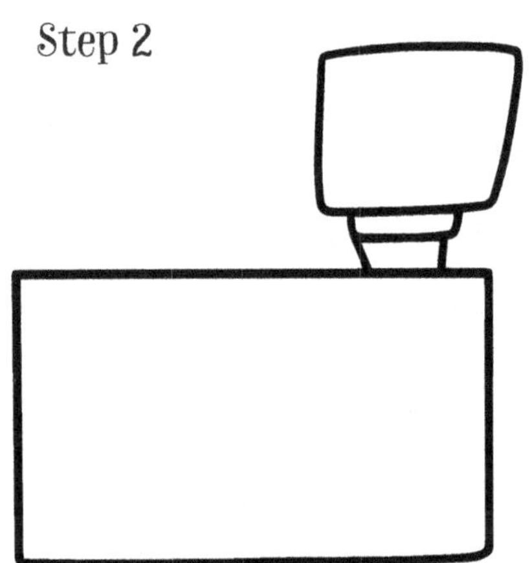

2. With a drawing pen trace over your pencil drawing. Draw a smaller rectangle at the top right to create a camera with a flash.

3. With a pen add lines to the top, bottom, and sides of the camera. Add three circles to the center of the camera to make the lens.

Step 3

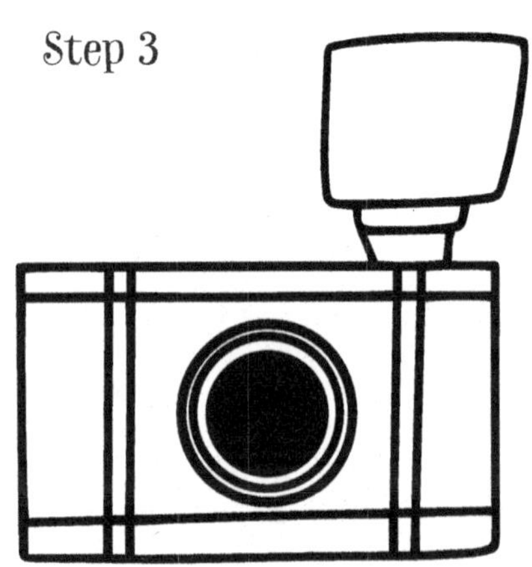

4. Finish the drawing by adding a view finder, shutter button, and winding button. Add accent lines in the flash and on the side of the camera. Draw a heart in the flash.

Step 4

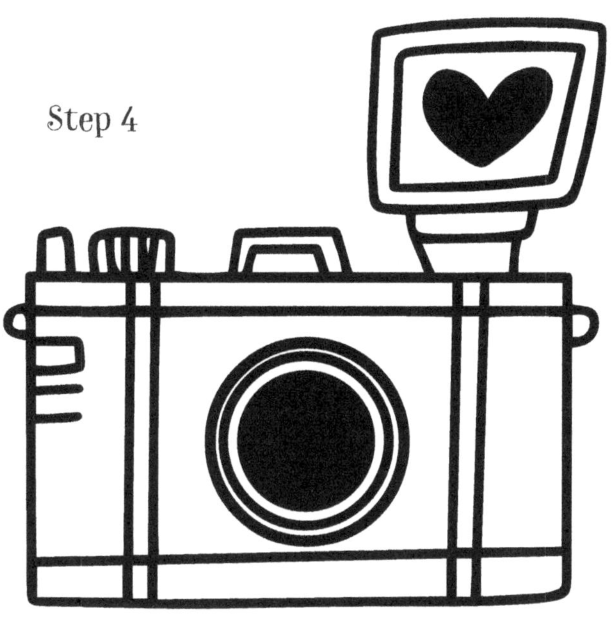

Draw your vintage camera below:

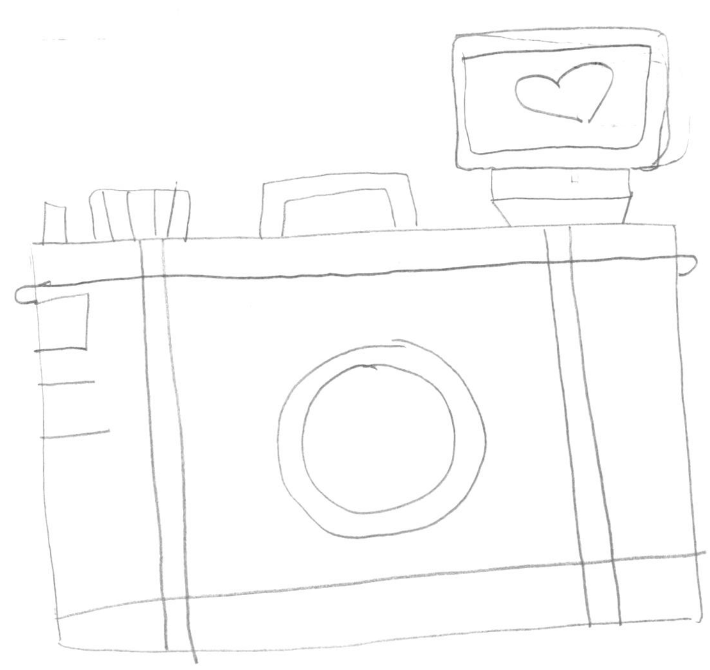

Let's draw a
teapot

Step 1

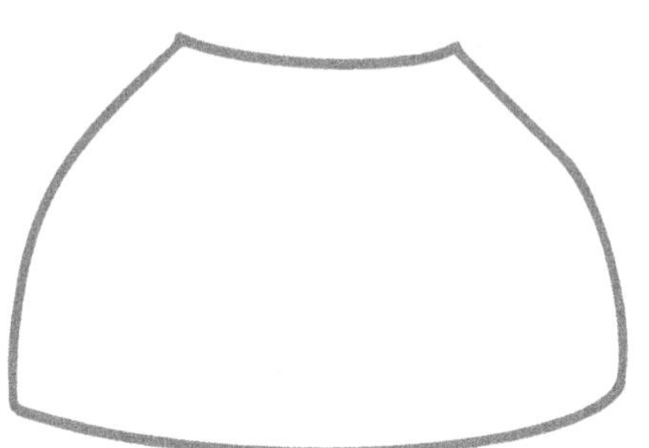

1. With a pencil draw the body of the teapot.

Step 2

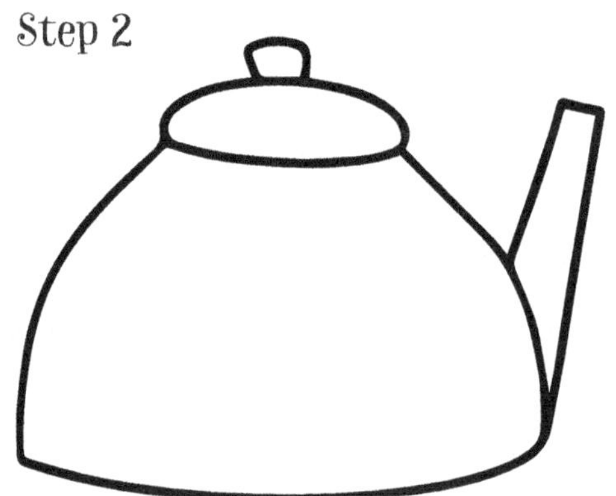

2. With a drawing pen trace over your pencil drawing. Draw a lid and a spout on the teapot.

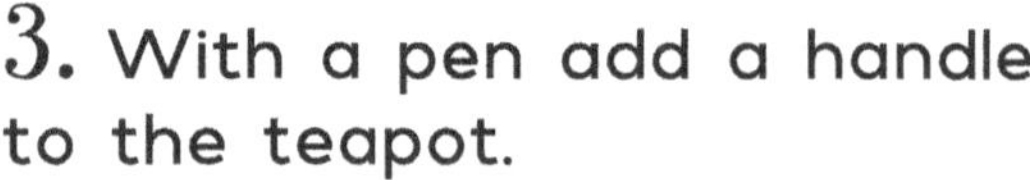

3. With a pen add a handle to the teapot.

Step 3

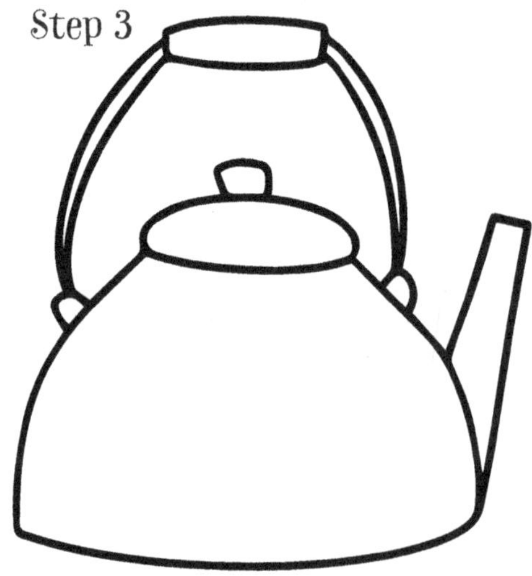

4. Finish the teapot by adding a scallop design at the top and bottom and steam coming out the spout.

Step 4

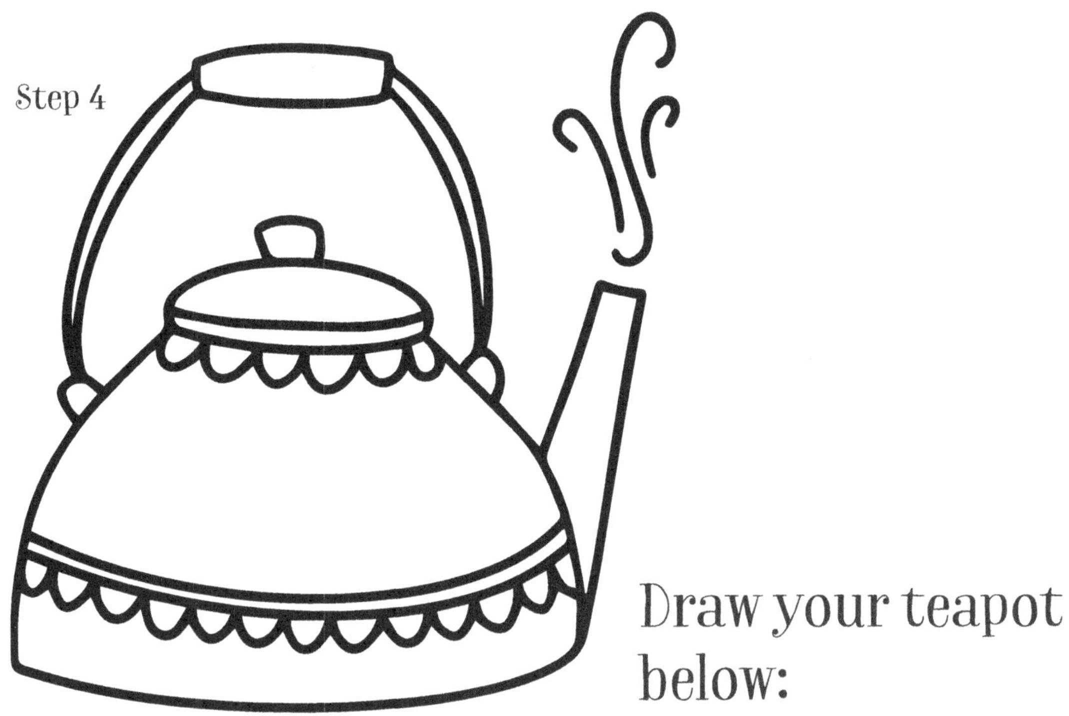

Draw your teapot below:

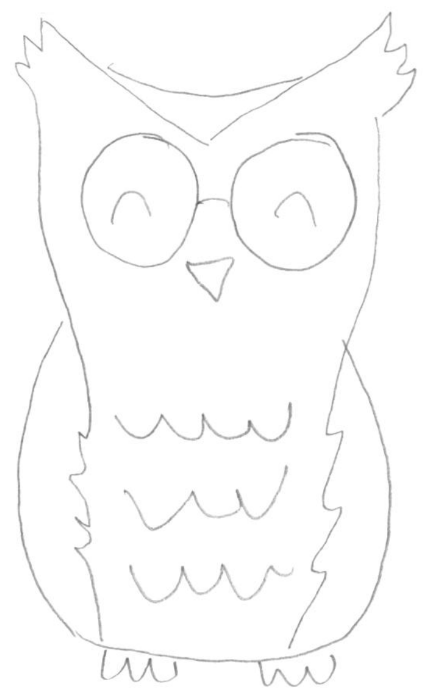

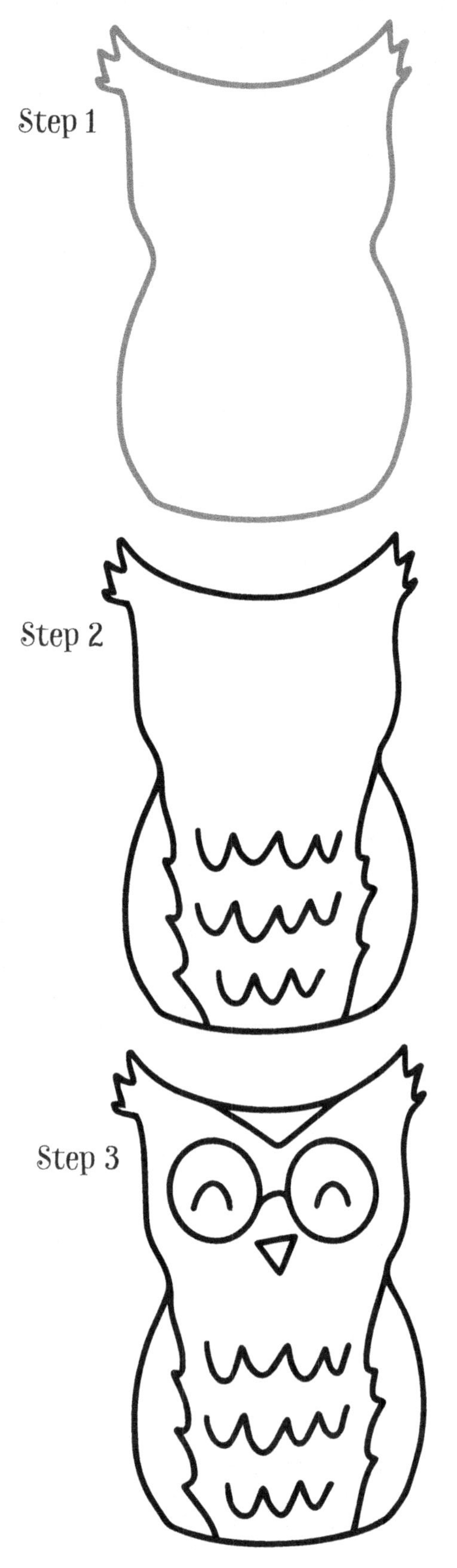

Let's draw an owl

1. With a pencil draw an owl.

2. With a drawing pen trace over your pencil drawing. Draw two wings on each side and lines of feathers on the belly of the owl.

3. With a pen add a triangle at the top of the owl's head. Draw eyeglasses, eyes, and a beak.

4. Finish the drawing by adding the owl's feet and a branch with leaves.

Step 4

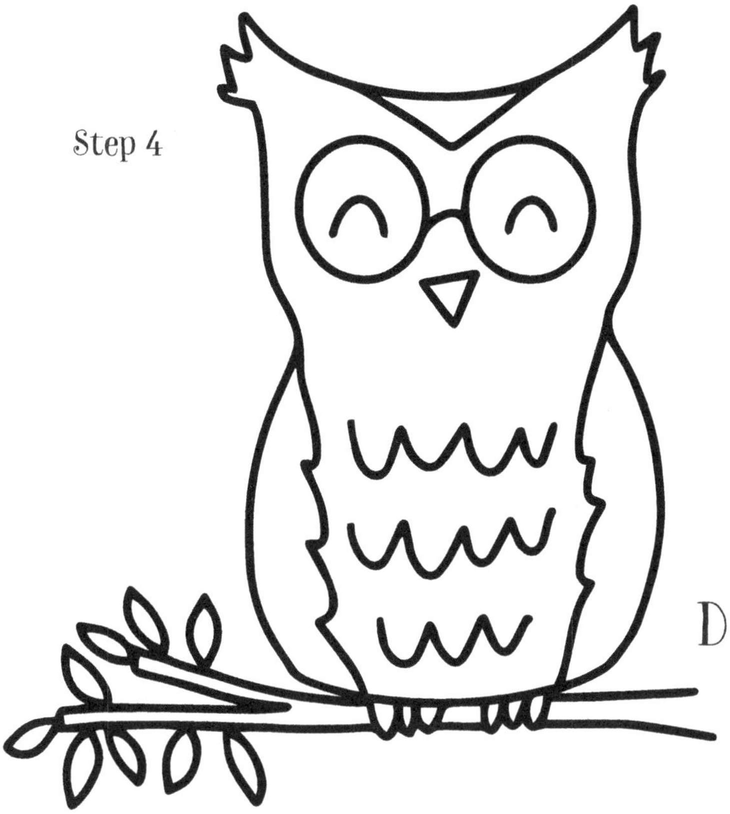

Draw your owl below:

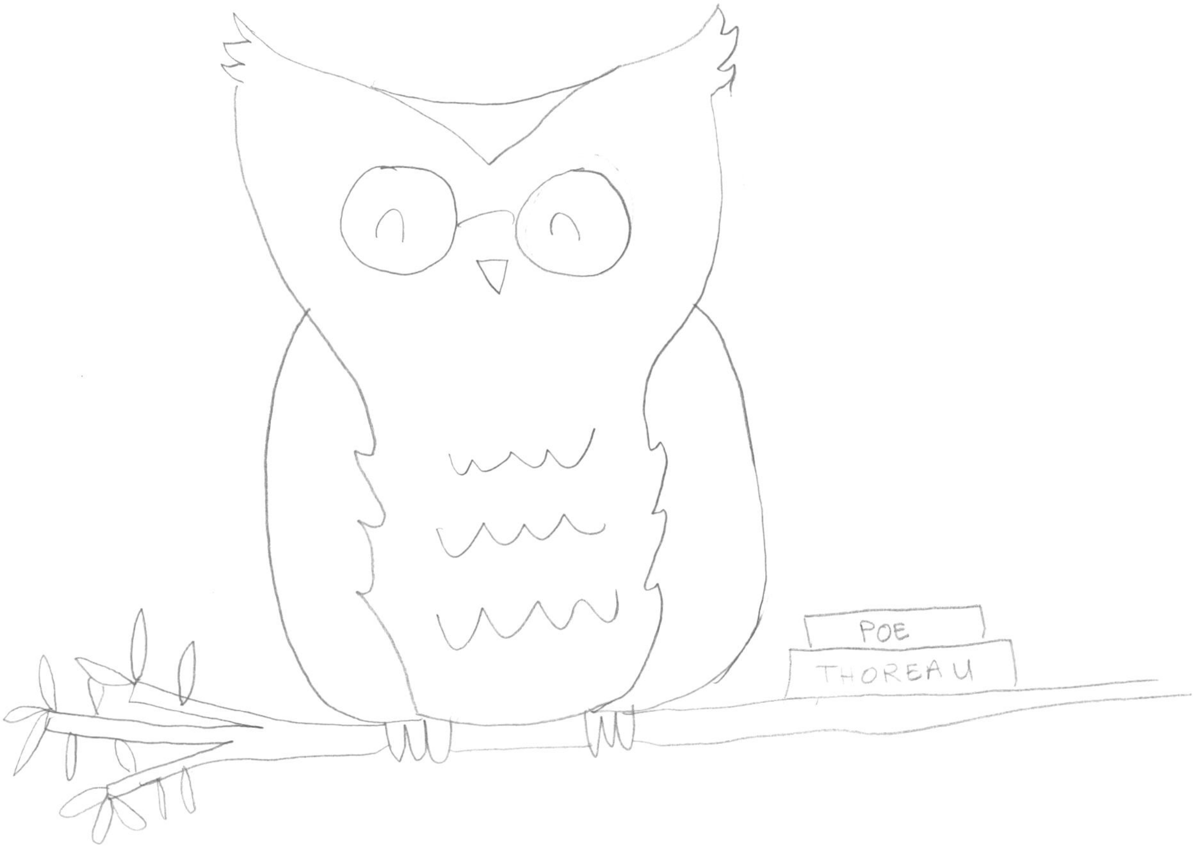

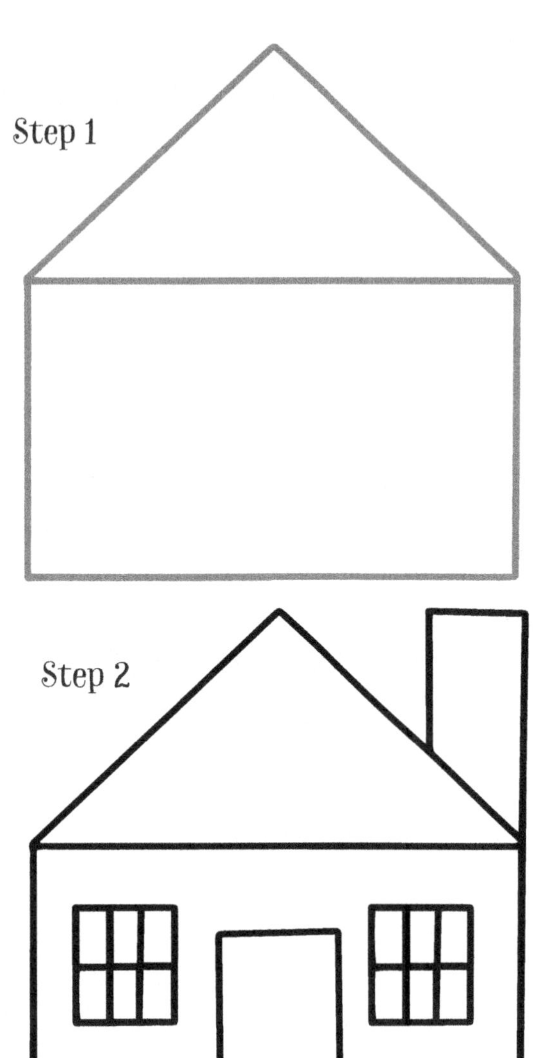

Let's draw a

house

1. With a pencil draw rectangle with a connecting triangle to create a house.

2. With a drawing pen trace over your pencil drawing. Draw a chimney, front door, and two windows.

3. With a pen add a doorknob, a little vent in the roof, and an awning above the door.

4. Finish the drawing by adding bushes under the windows, bricks in the chimney, and little reflection lines on window panes.

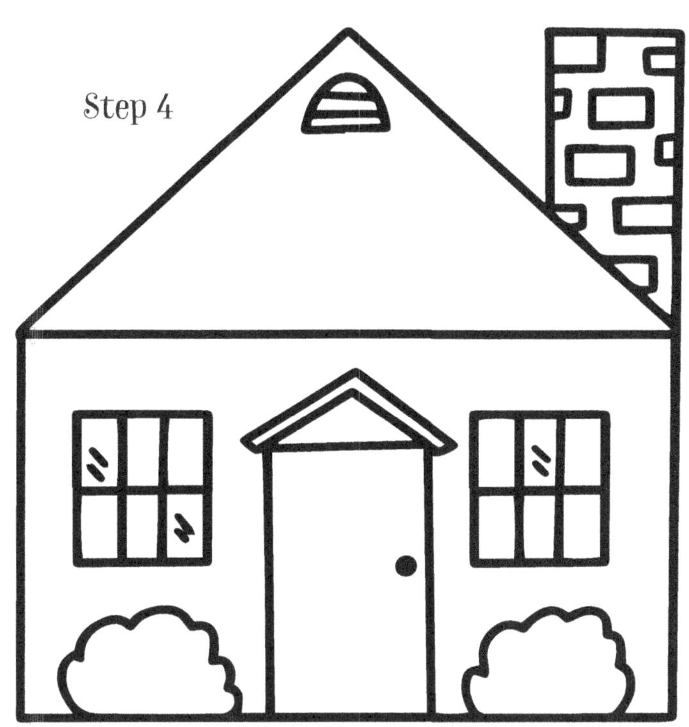

Draw your house below:

Step 1

Let's draw a

bicycle

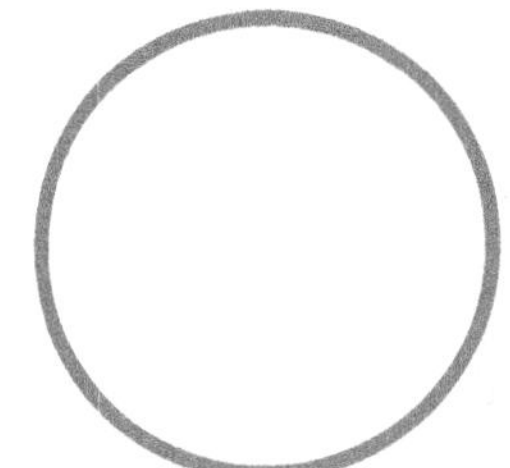

1. With a pencil draw two parallel circles.

Step 2

2. With a drawing pen trace over your pencil drawing. Draw lines crossing in the center to create spokes of two bicycle tires.

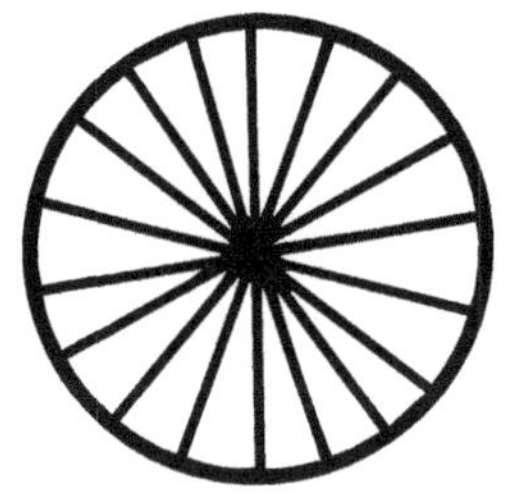

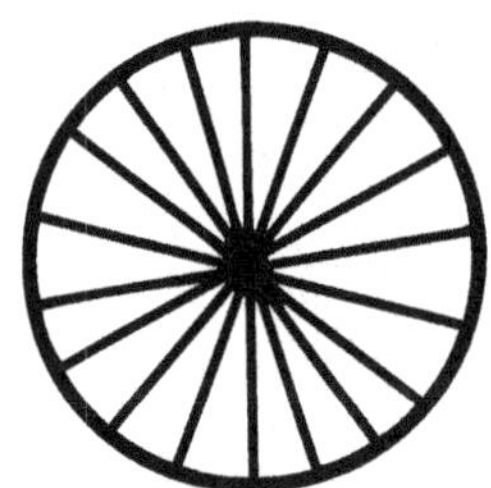

3. With a pen add a bicycle frame connecting both tires.

Step 3

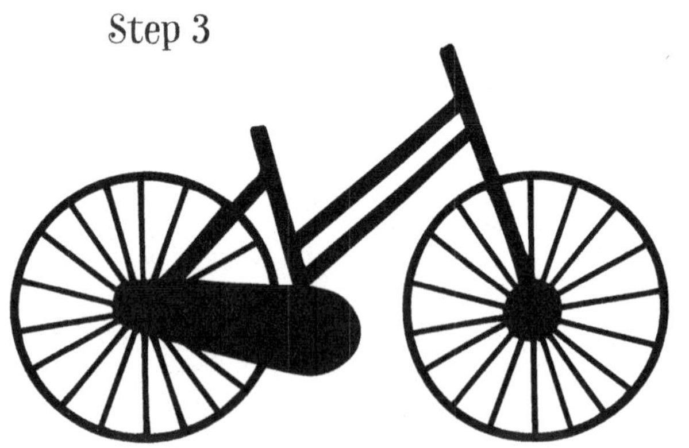

4. Finish the bicycle by drawing a seat, handlebar, and basket.

Step 4

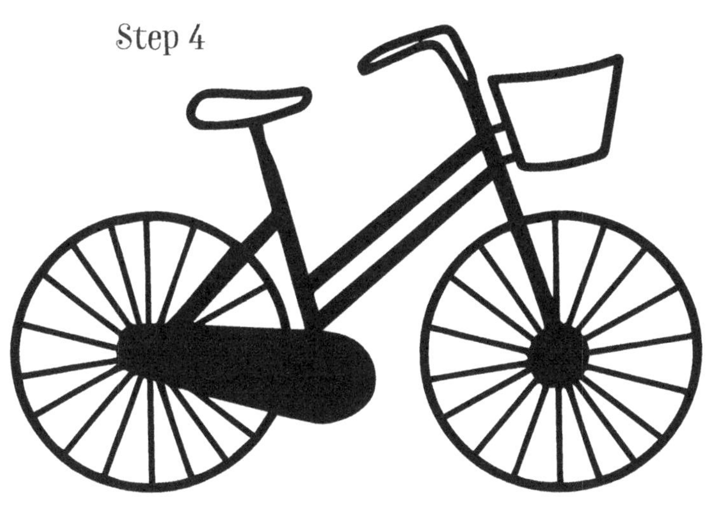

Draw your bicycle below:

Let's draw a

mushroom

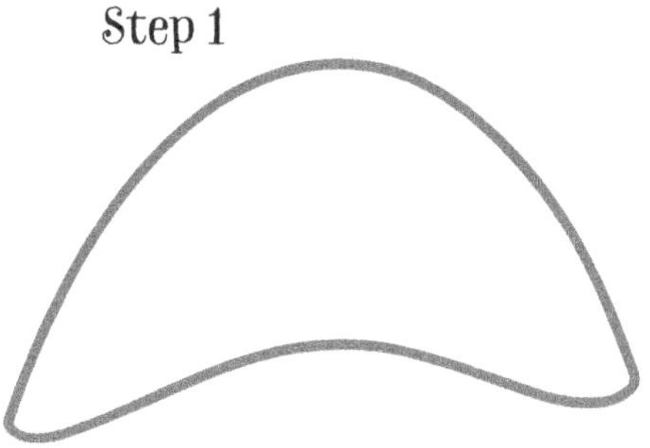

1. With a pencil draw a half circle with a curved bottom side.

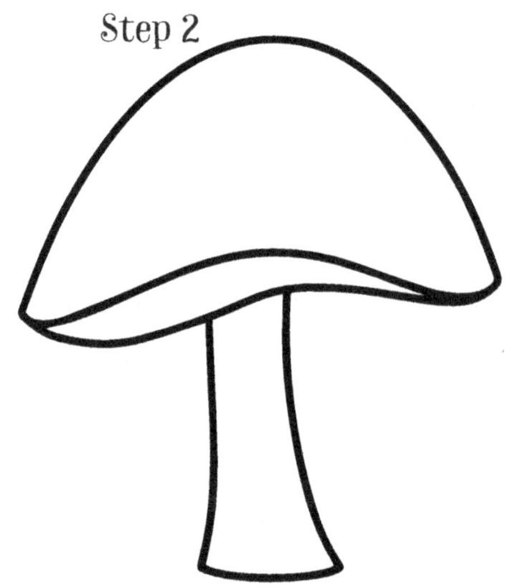

2. With a drawing pen trace over your pencil drawing. Draw another curved line and a stem to create a mushroom.

3. With a pen a row of vertical lines in the underside of the mushroom cap.

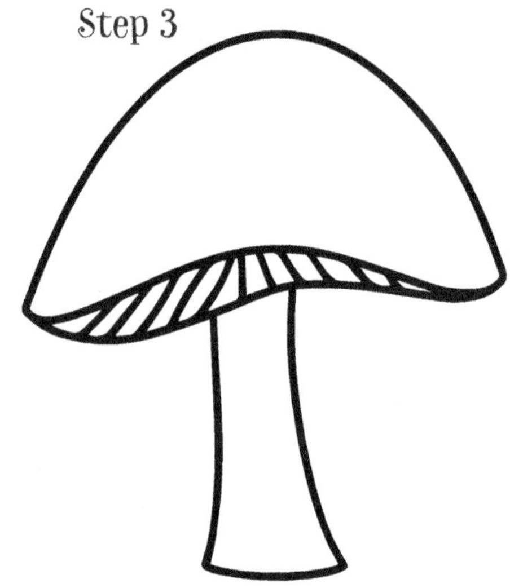

4. Finish the mushroom by drawing polka-dots on the top side of the cap. Add blades of grass around the bottom of the stem.

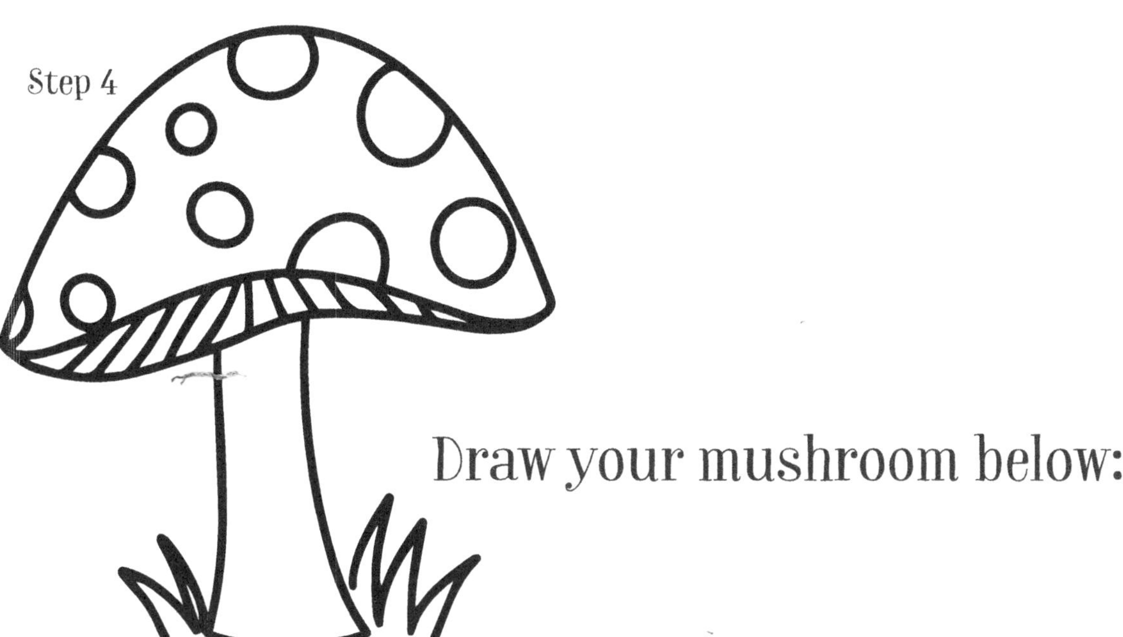

Draw your mushroom below:

Let's draw a

happy sunshine

Step 1

1. With a pencil draw a fluffy cloud with arches varying in size.

Step 2

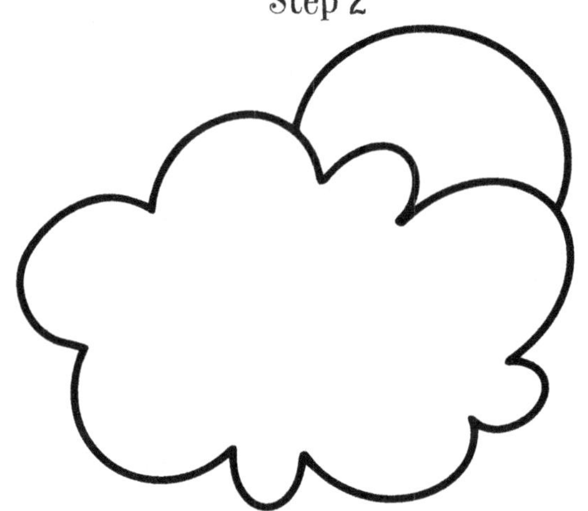

2. With a drawing pen trace over your pencil drawing. Add a sun by creating a half circle at the top right side of the cloud.

Step 3

3. With a pen add rays of sunshine along the edges of the sun.

4. Finish the drawing by adding eyes and a smile to the cloud.

Step 4

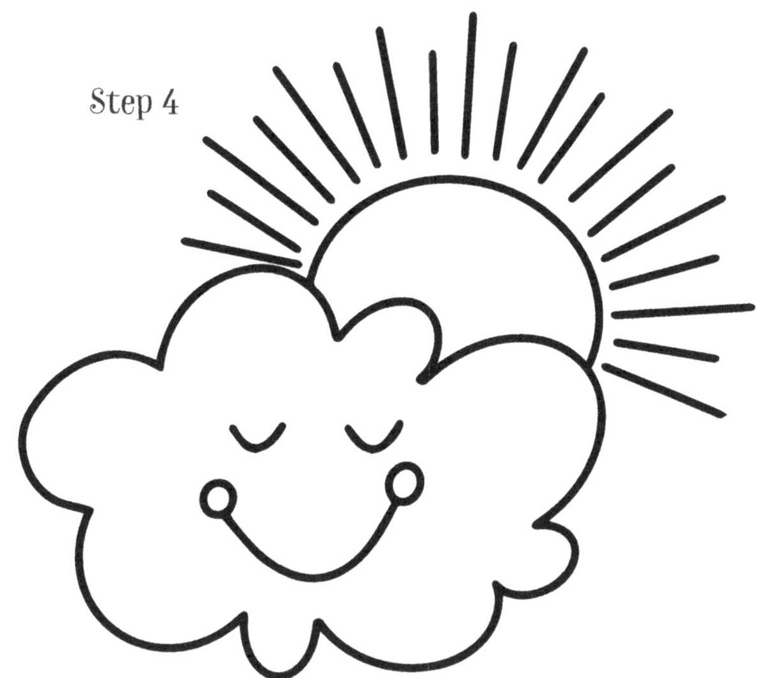

Draw your happy sunshine below:

Step 1

Let's draw a **acorn**

1. With a pencil draw the top of an acorn.

Step 2

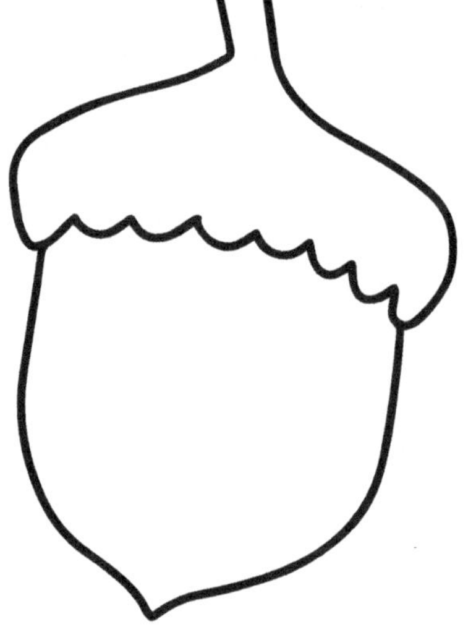

2. With a drawing pen trace over your pencil drawing. Add the nut part of the acorn.

Step 3

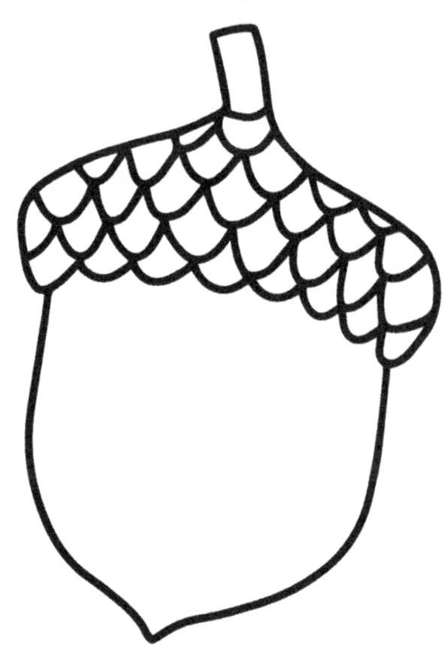

3. With a pen add scallops in the top of the acorn.

4. Finish the drawing by adding a little branch attached to the top of the acorn.

Step 4

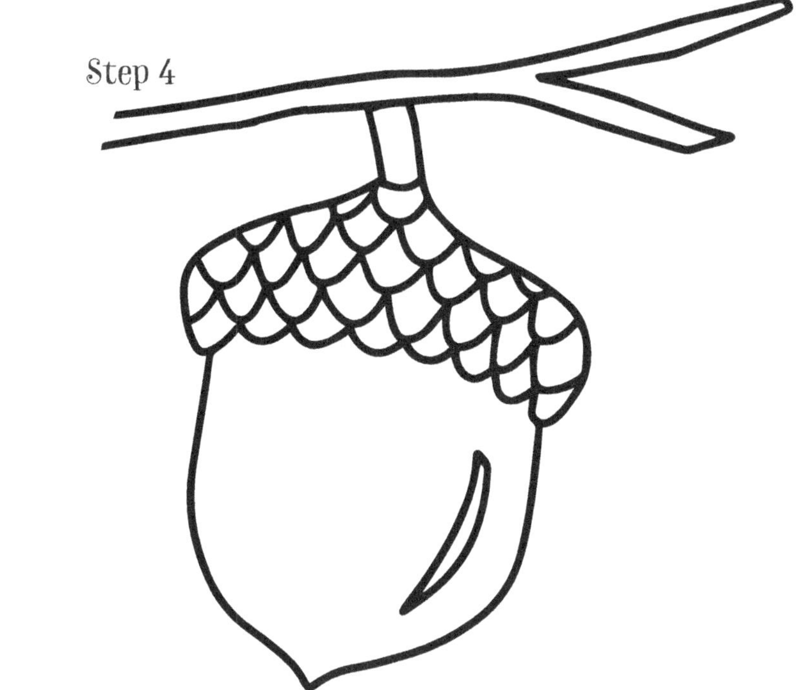

Draw your acorn below:

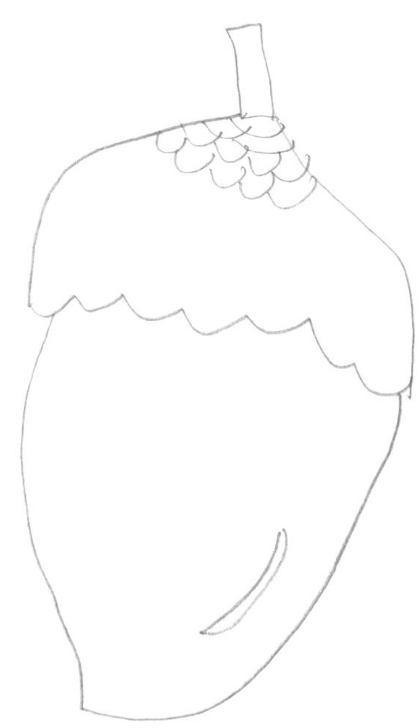

Let's draw a

daisy

Step 1

1. With a pencil draw a small circle to create the center of a daisy.

Step 2

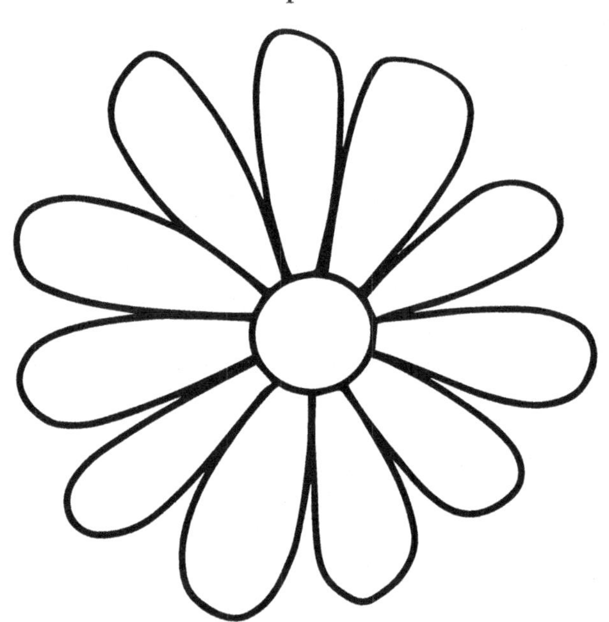

2. With a drawing pen trace over your pencil drawing. Add petals all around the center.

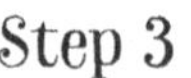

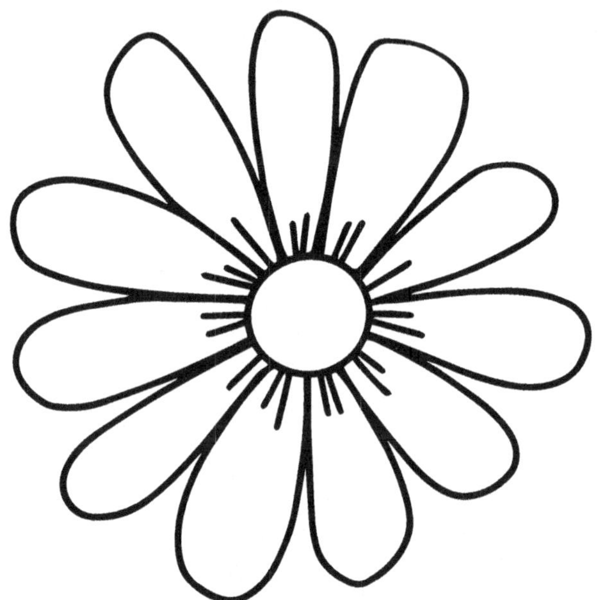

3. With a pen add small accent lines from the center on each petal.

4. Finish the drawing by adding texture to the center of the daisy and accent leaves.

Draw your daisy below:

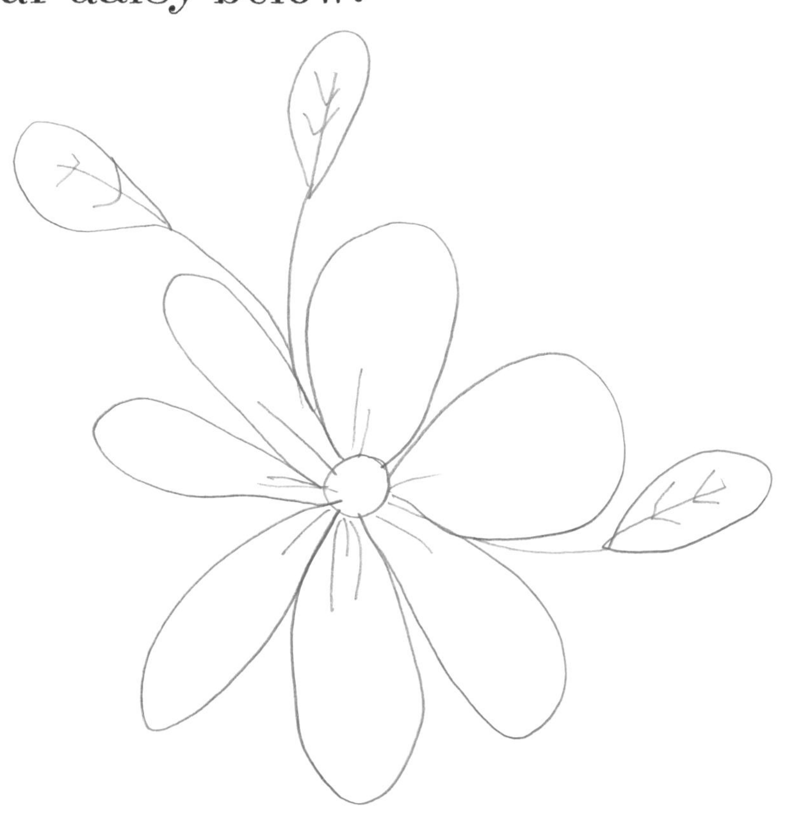

Let's draw a

French fries

Step 1

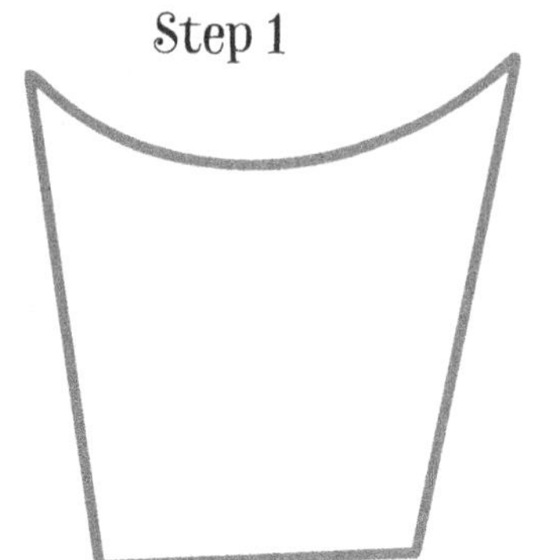

1. With a pencil draw a box for French fries.

Step 2

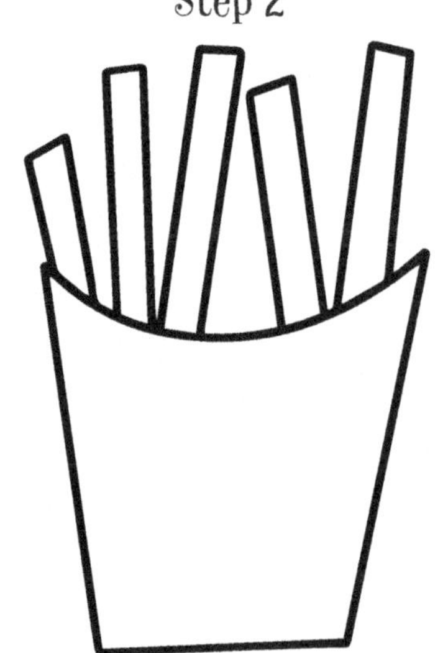

2. With a drawing pen trace over your pencil drawing. Add a layer of french fries coming out of the top of the box.

Step 3

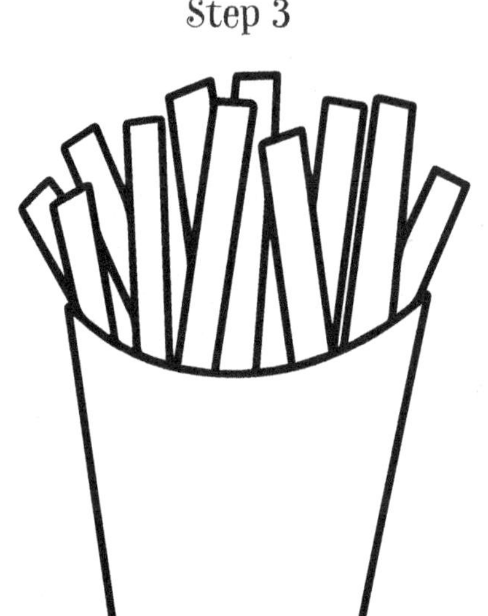

3. With a pen add a second layer of French fries.

4. Finish the drawing by adding a happy face and lines at the top and bottom of the box.

Step 4

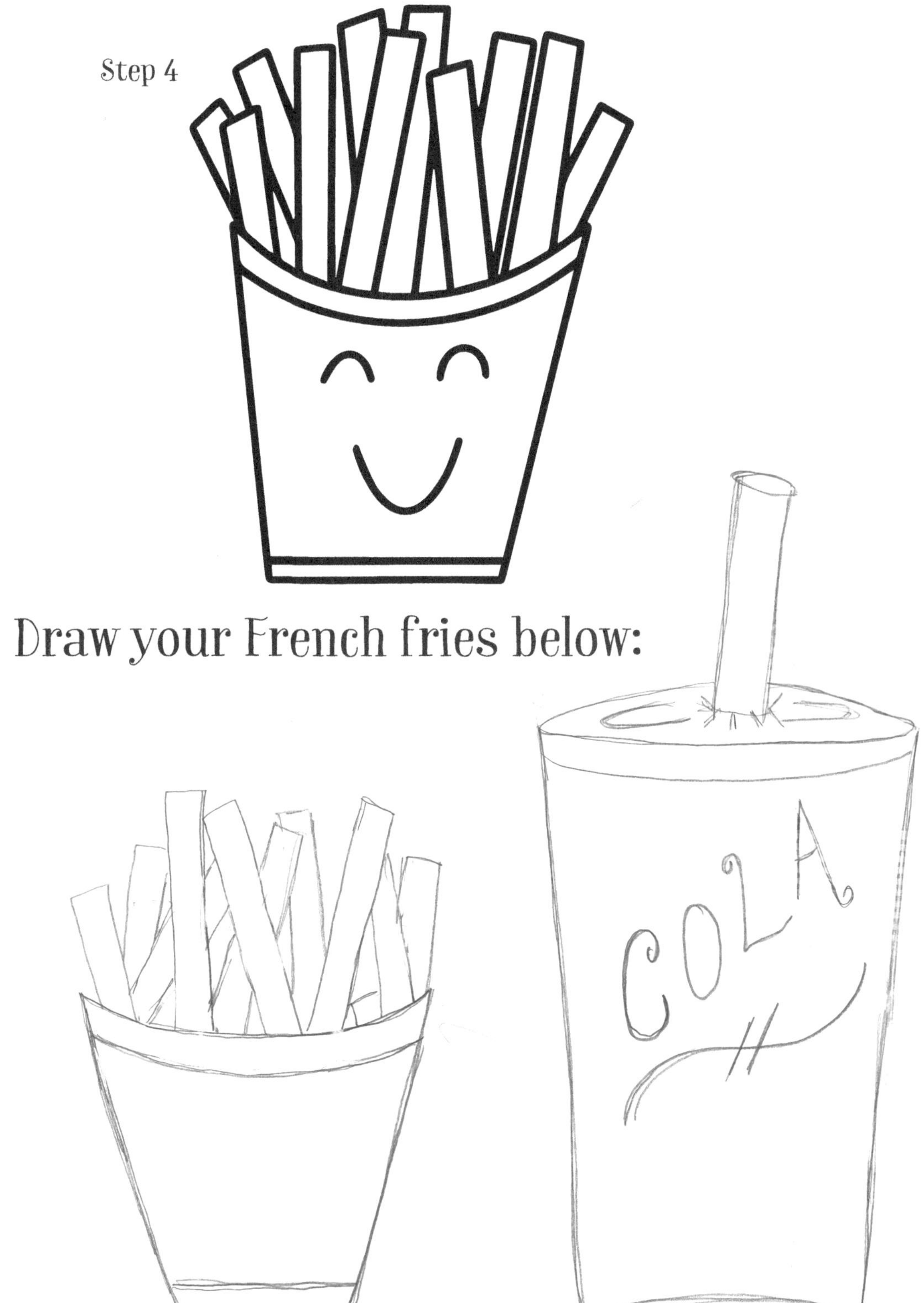

Draw your French fries below:

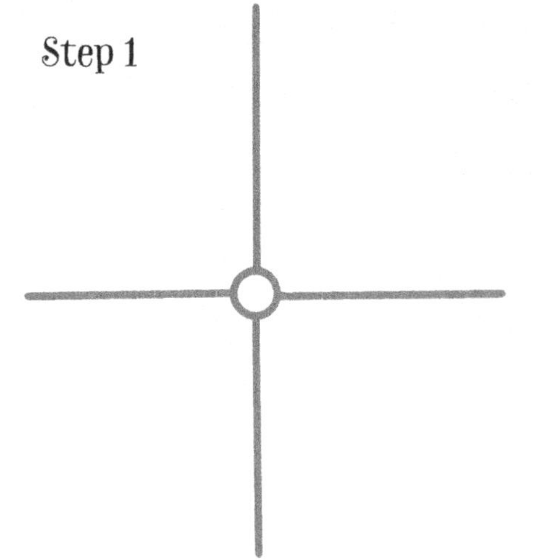

Let's draw a

snowflake

1. With a pencil draw an small circle with two lines crossed.

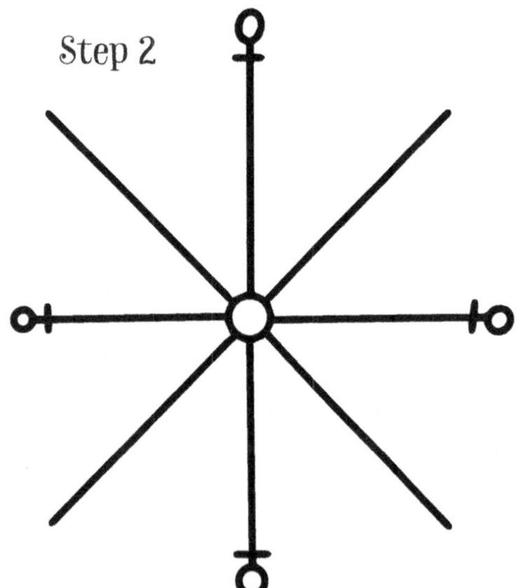

2. With a drawing pen trace over your pencil drawing. Add accent circles and lines at the top of the crossed lines.
Add angled lines from the center of the crossed lines.

3. With a pen continue to add small circles and accent lines to form a snowflake.

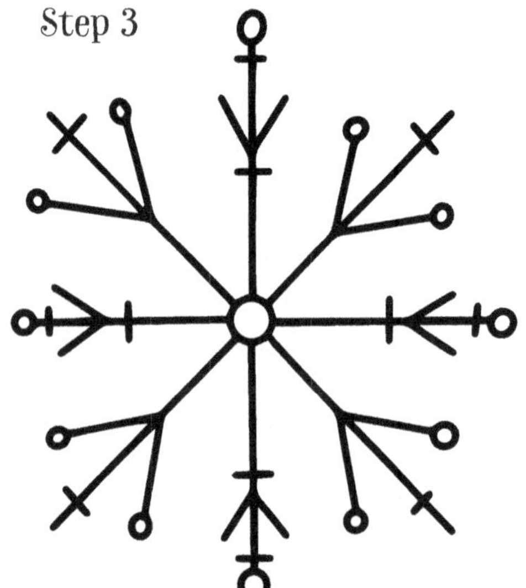

4. Finish the snowflake by drawing additional detailed lines, circles, and half circles.

Step 4

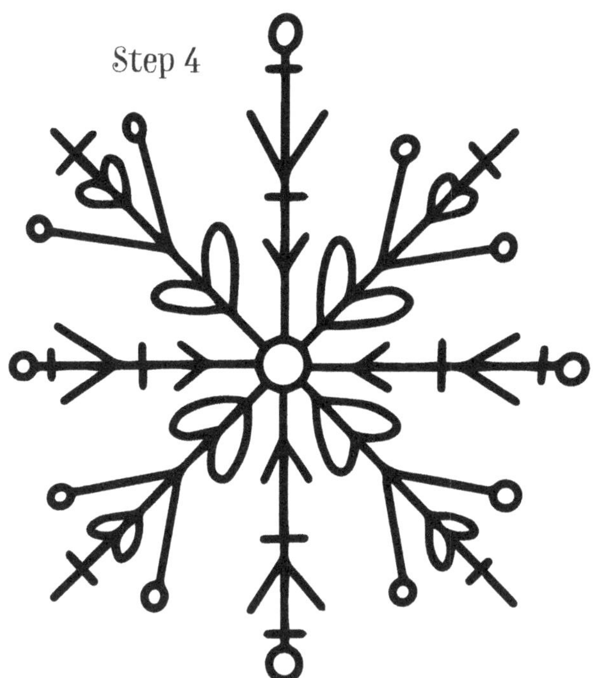

Draw your snowflake below:

Let's draw a cake

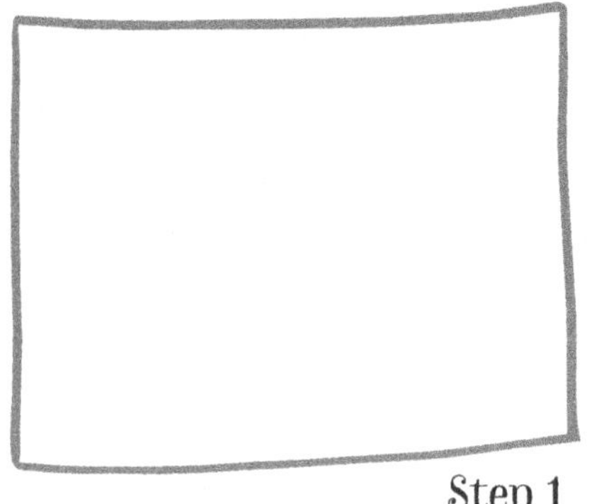

Step 1

1. With a pencil draw the outline of the cake.

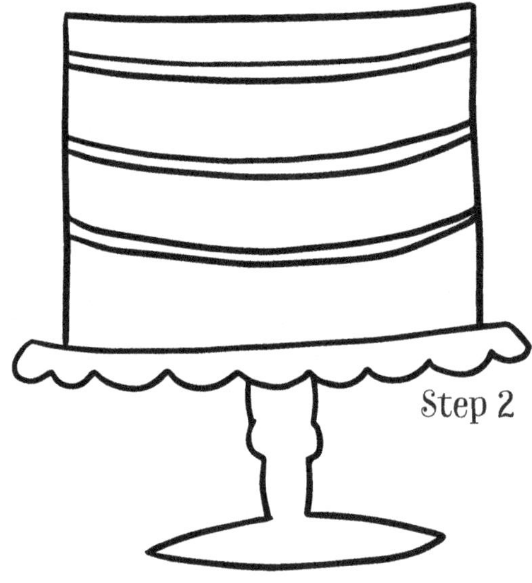

Step 2

2. With a drawing pen trace over your pencil sketch. Add layers to the cake. Under the cake draw a cake stand.

3. With a pen add scallop details under each layer.

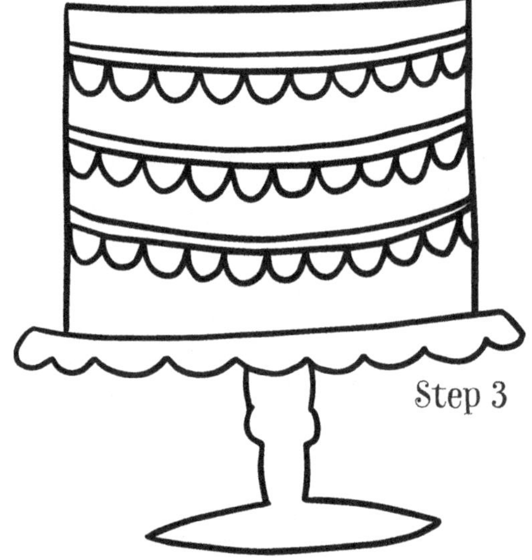

Step 3

4. Finish the by adding candles on top of the cake.

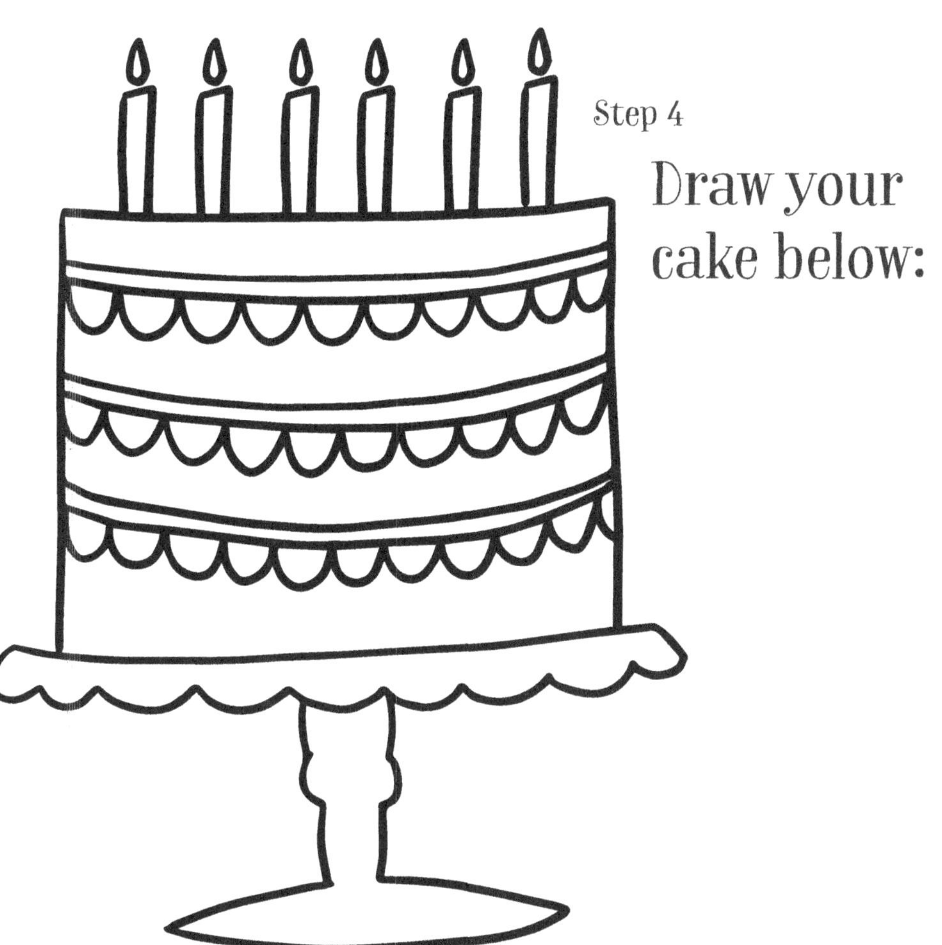

Step 4

Draw your cake below:

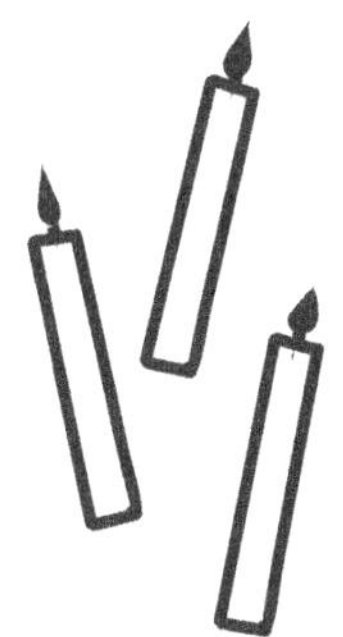

Let's draw a chicken

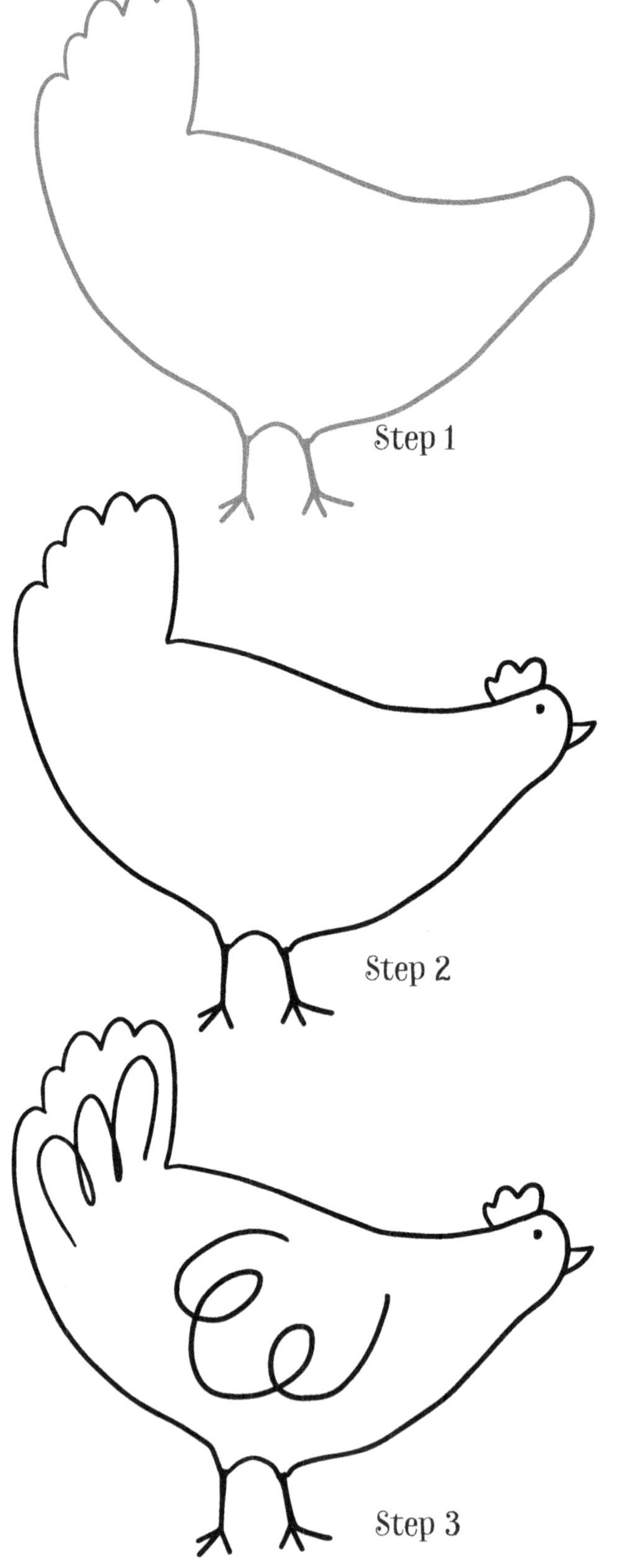

1. With a pencil draw the body of the chicken including the tail feathers and feet.

2. With a drawing pen trace over your pencil sketch. Add lines to form the chicken's comb, beak, and dot for its eye.

3. With a pen add looping lines to create feather details and wing.

4. Finish your drawing by adding grass details.

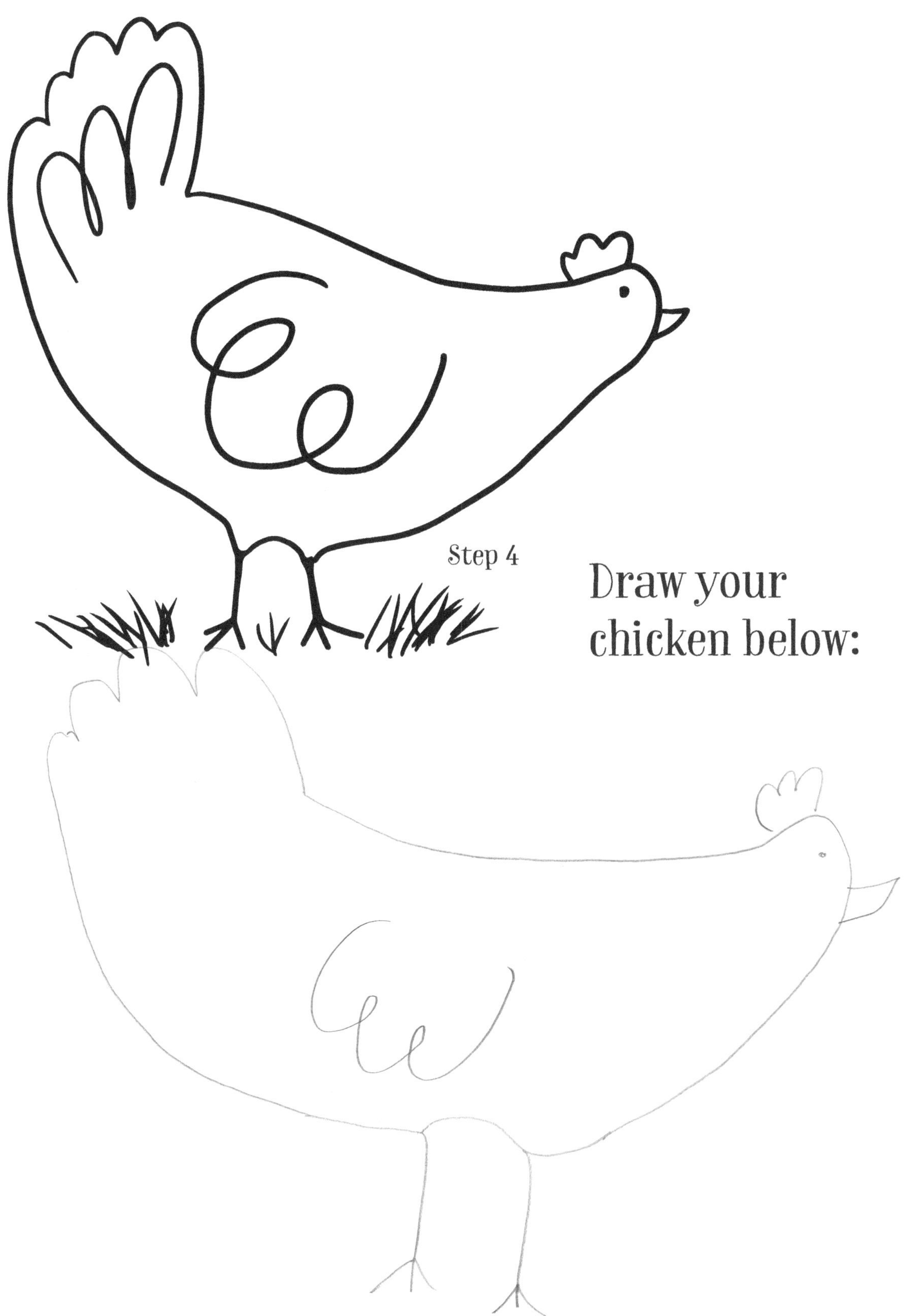

Step 4

Draw your chicken below:

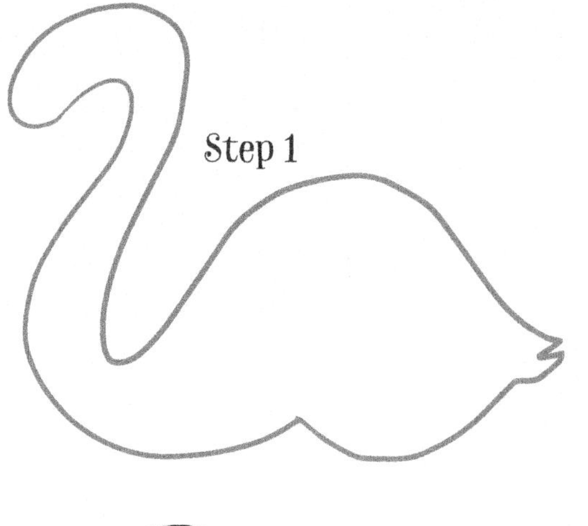

Let's draw a

flamingo

1. With a pencil draw the body of the flamingo, adding a long curved neck and a tail.

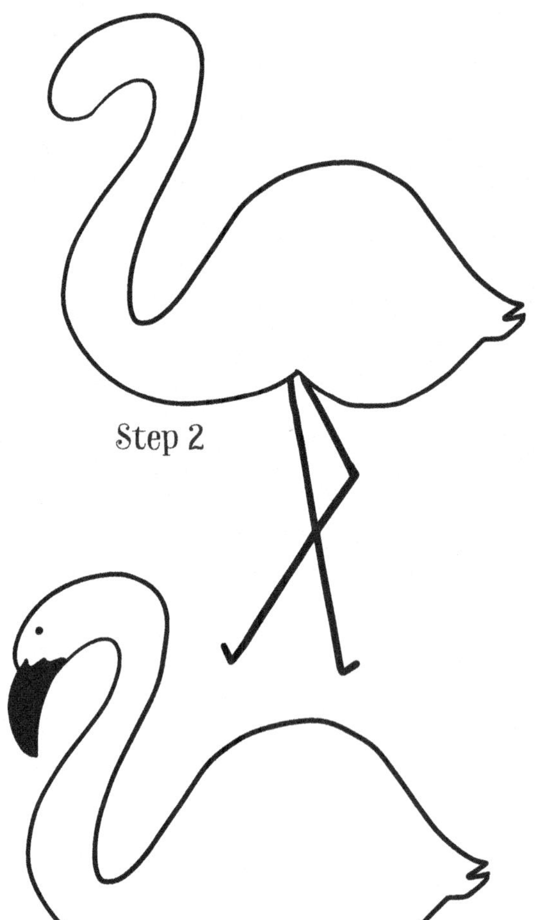

2. With a drawing pen trace over your pencil sketch. Add lines to form the flamingo's legs.

3. With a pen add a dot for its eye and then add a curved bill.

Step 3

4. Finish the flamingo by adding layers of curved lines for the wing feathers.

Step 4

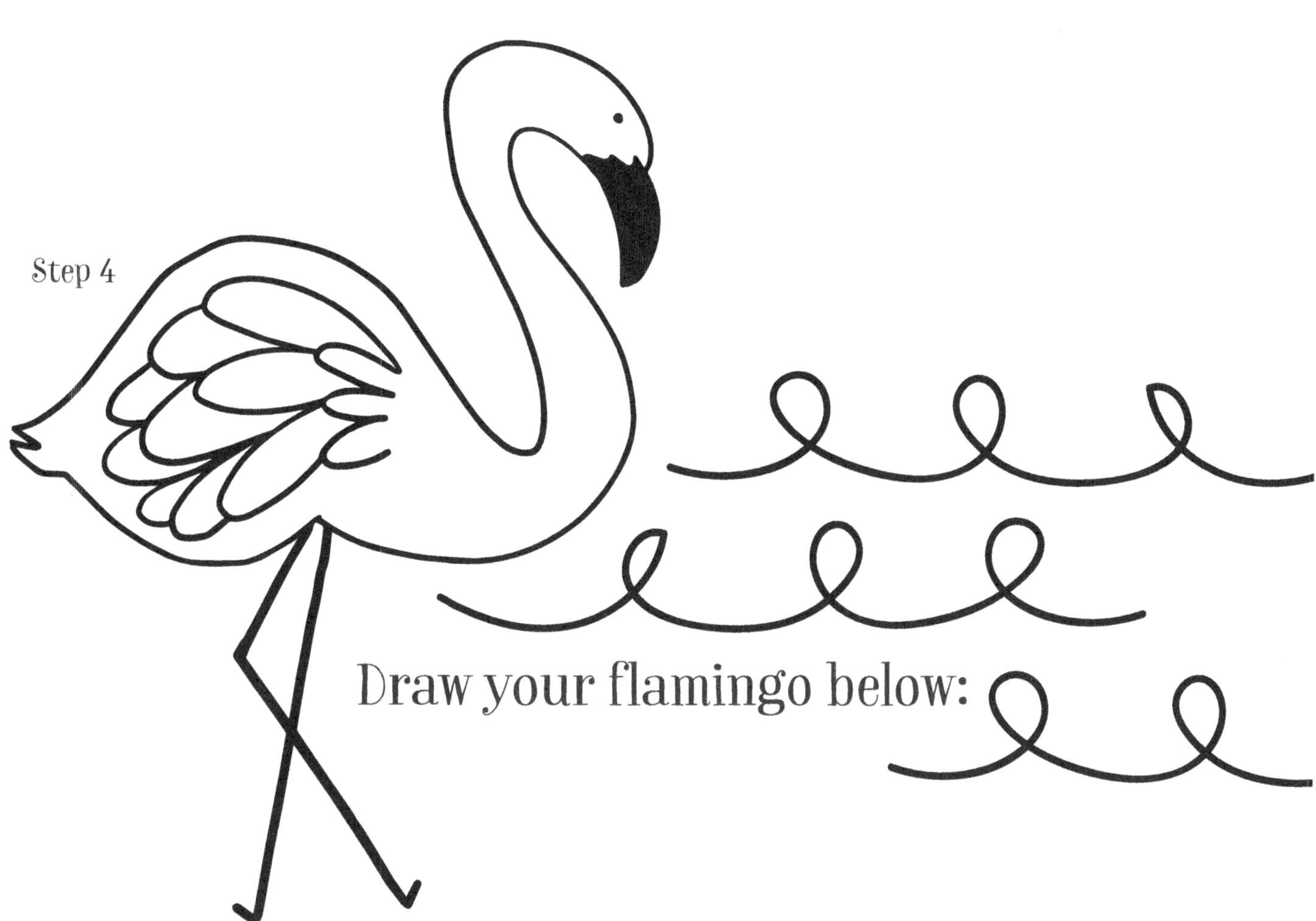

Draw your flamingo below:

let's draw a

honey bee

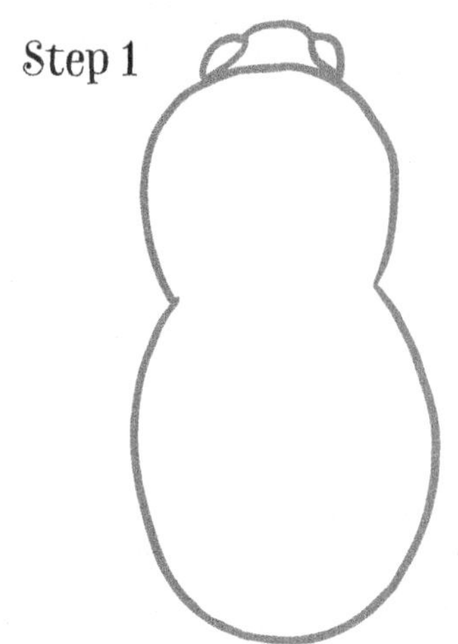

1. With a pencil draw two ovals connecting one on top of the other to form the body of the honey bee. At the top add the bee's head & eyes.

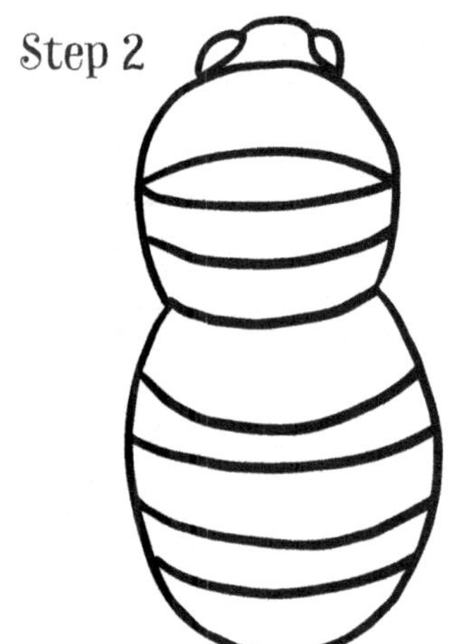

2. With a drawing pen trace over your pencil drawing. Add in the bee's stripes on the body

3. With a pen add wings on each side of the bee's body.

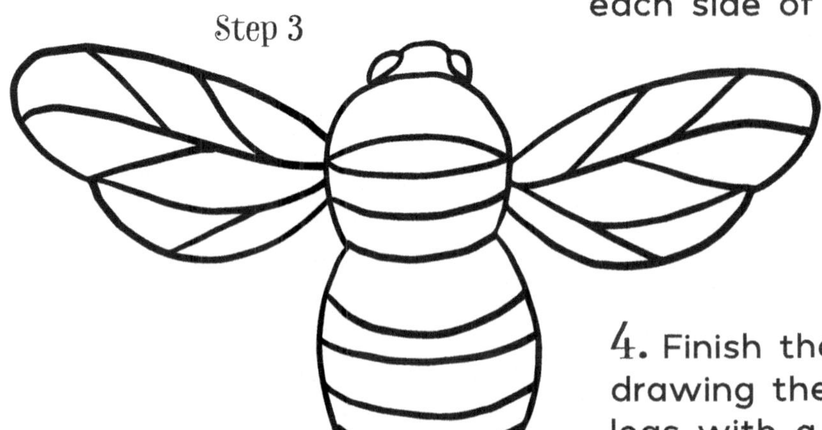

4. Finish the honey bee by drawing the antenea and legs with a pen.

Step 4

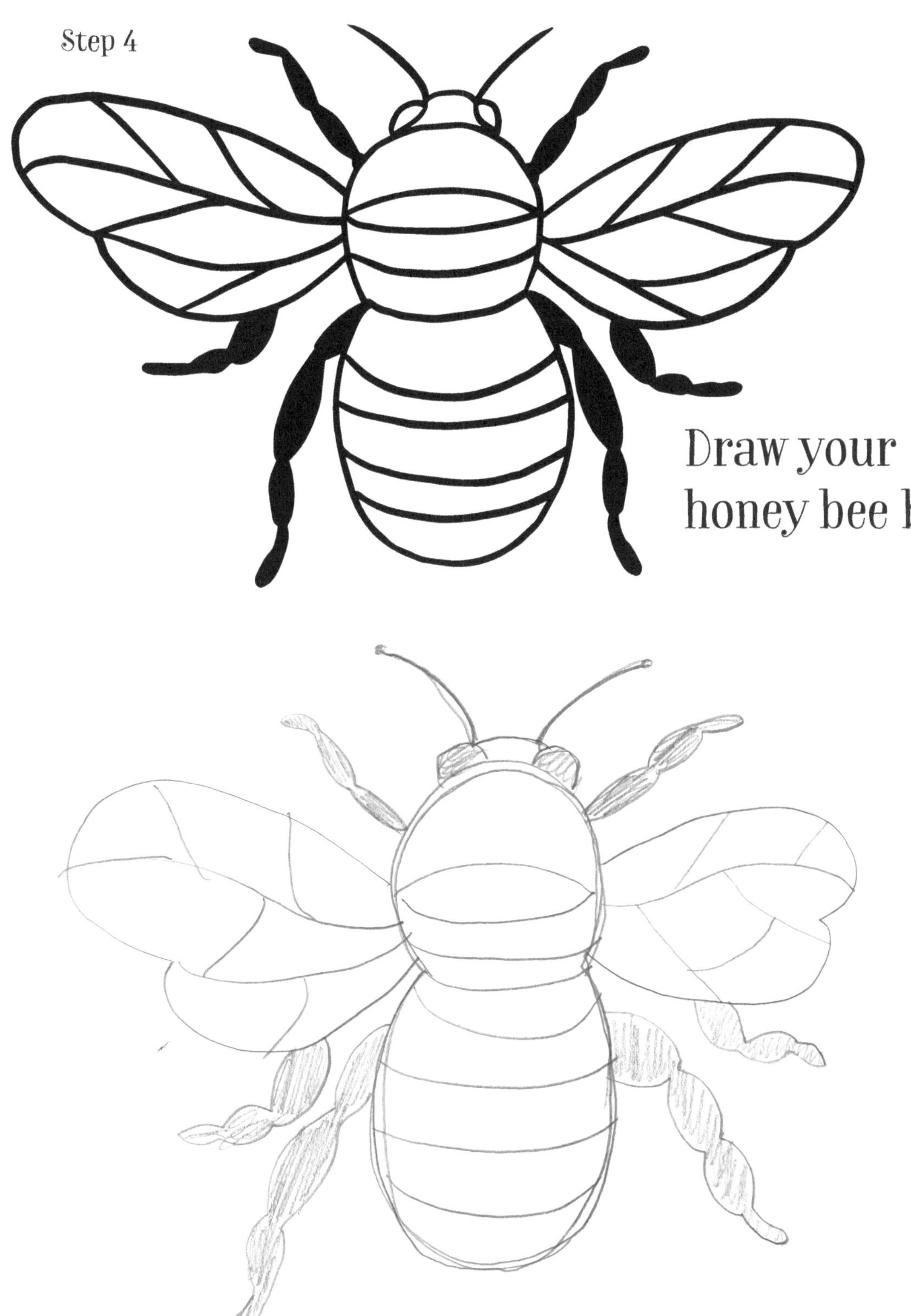

Draw your honey bee below:

Step 1

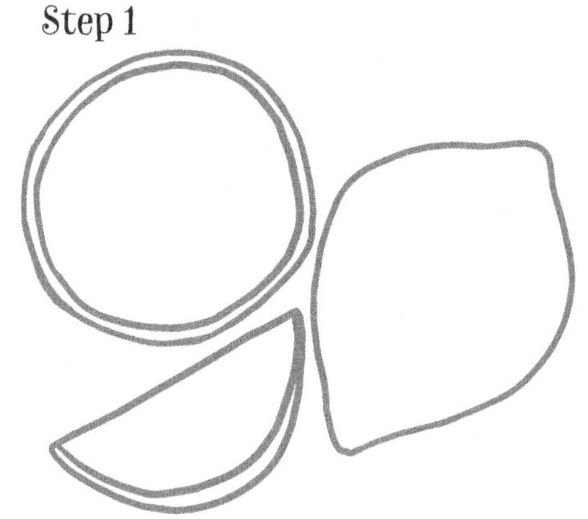

Let's draw lemons

1. With a pencil draw a whole lemon, a lemon slice, and a lemon wedge.

Step 2

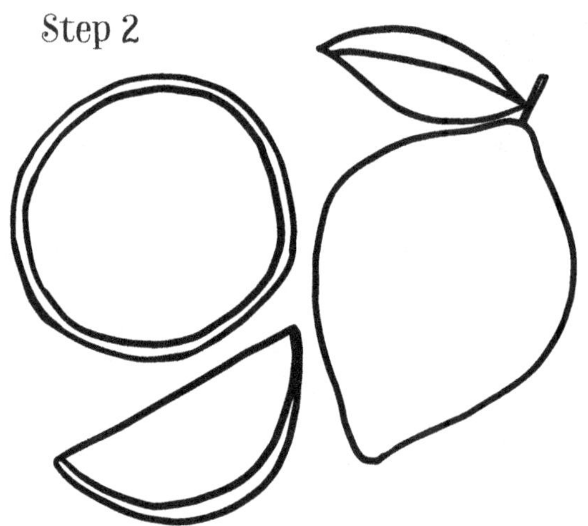

2. With a drawing pen trace over your pencil sketch. Add a stem and leaf to the whole lemon.

3. With a pen add in details on the lemon slice and lemon wedge.

Step 3

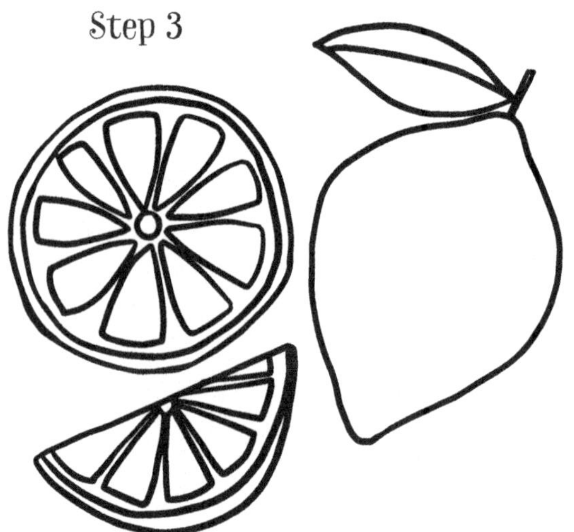

4. Finish the lemons by adding texture spots to the whole lemon.

Step 4

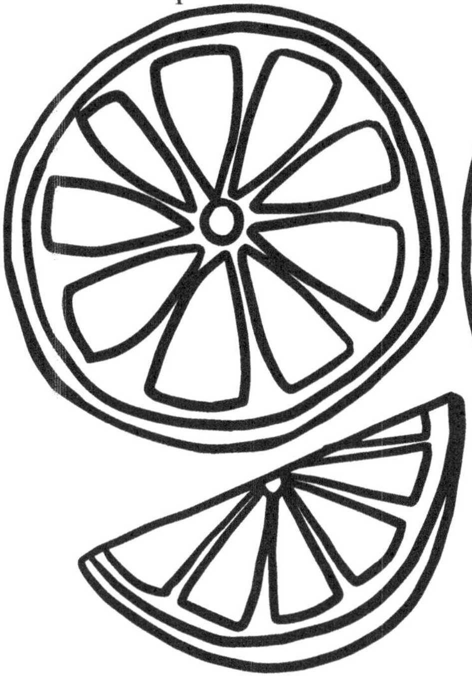

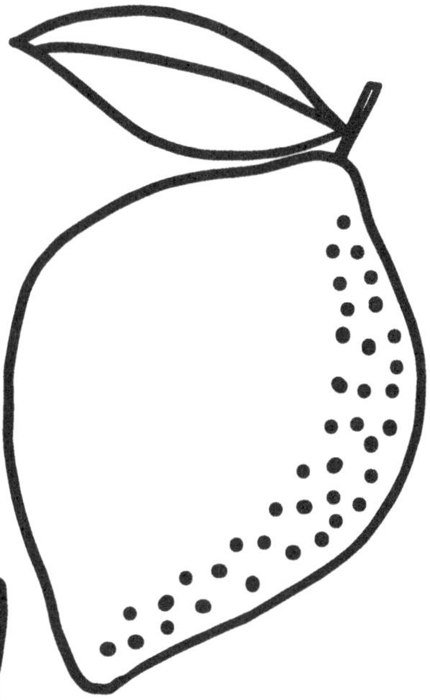

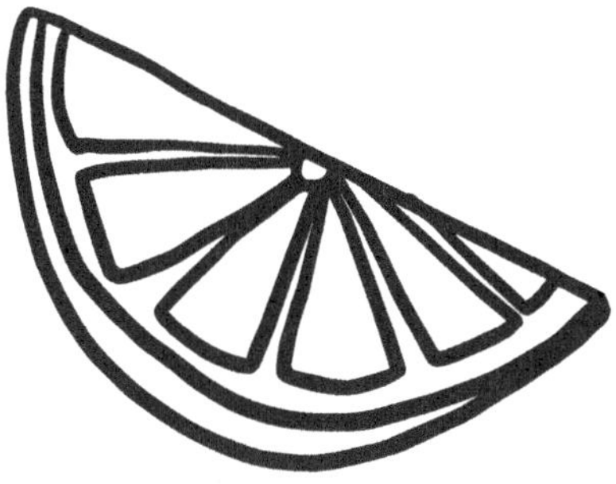

Draw your lemons below:

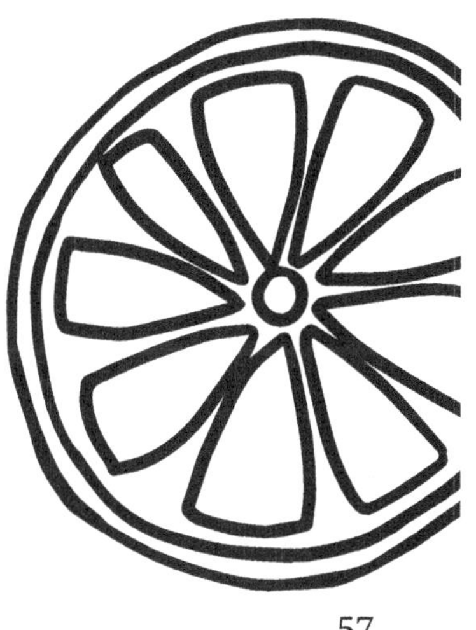

Let's draw a

glass of lemonade

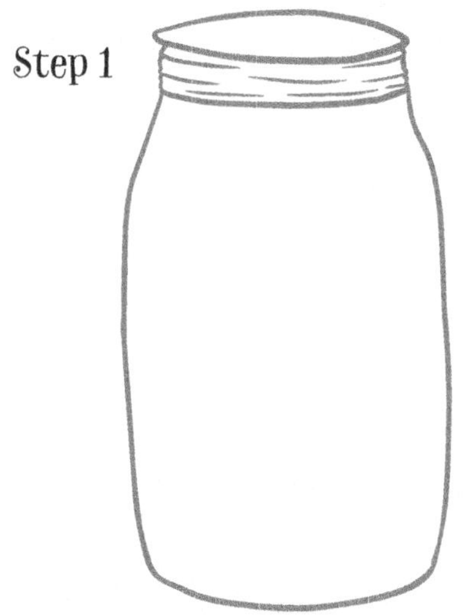

1. With a pencil draw a mason jar with an open top and rim details.

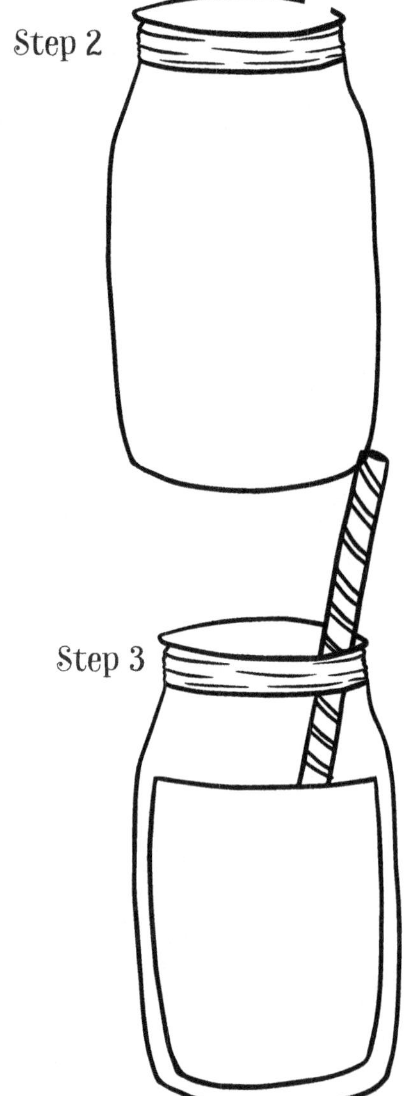

2. With a drawing pen trace over your pencil sketch leaving a small gap on one side of the jar where you'll add a straw.

3. With a pen add lemonade inside the jar and then draw a straw coming out of the liquid and going up through the top of the jar.

4. Finish the lemonade with ice cubes and a wedge of lemon on the side.

Step 4

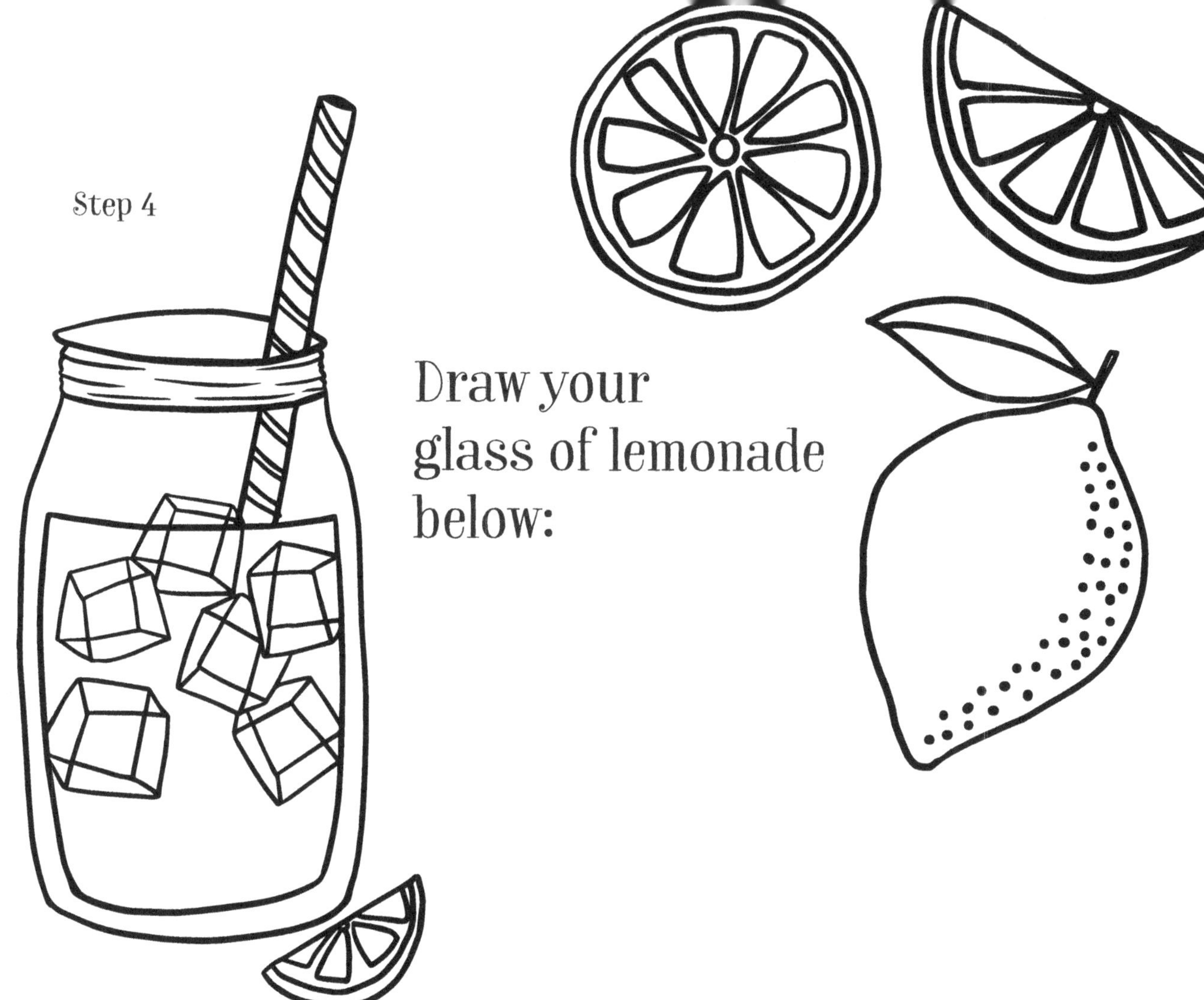

Draw your glass of lemonade below:

Step 1

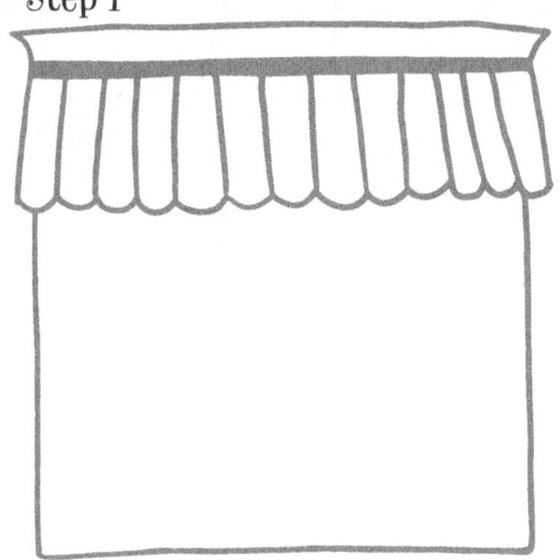

Let's draw a cute storefront

1. With a pencil draw the outline of a store front with a cute scalloped awning along the top of the building.

Step 2

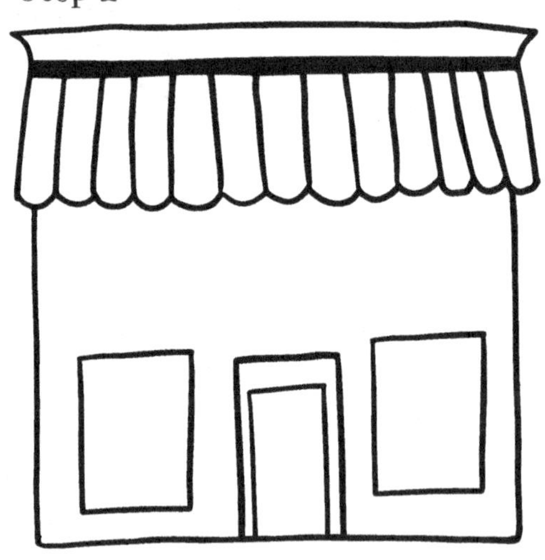

2. With a drawing pen trace over your pencil sketch. Add lines to form the door and windows.

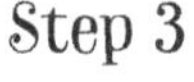

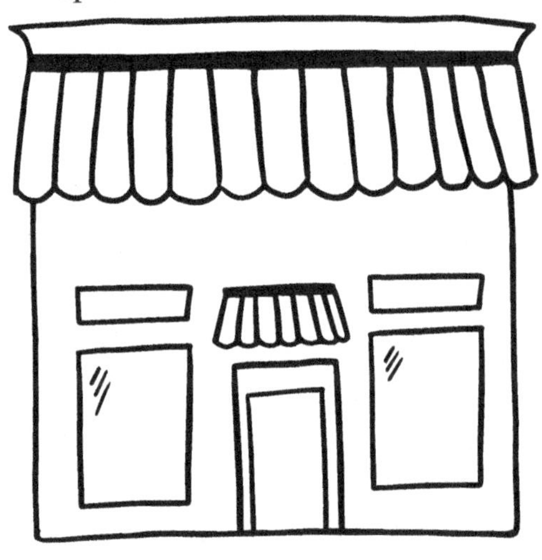

3. With a pen add smaller windows above the main windows. Add in little line details on the main windows, and draw a small entranc canopy above the door to match the scalloped awning.

4. Finish the storefront by adding a space for a sign above the entrance. Draw a sidewalk in front of the store, and add a little sign to the side of the store.

Step 4

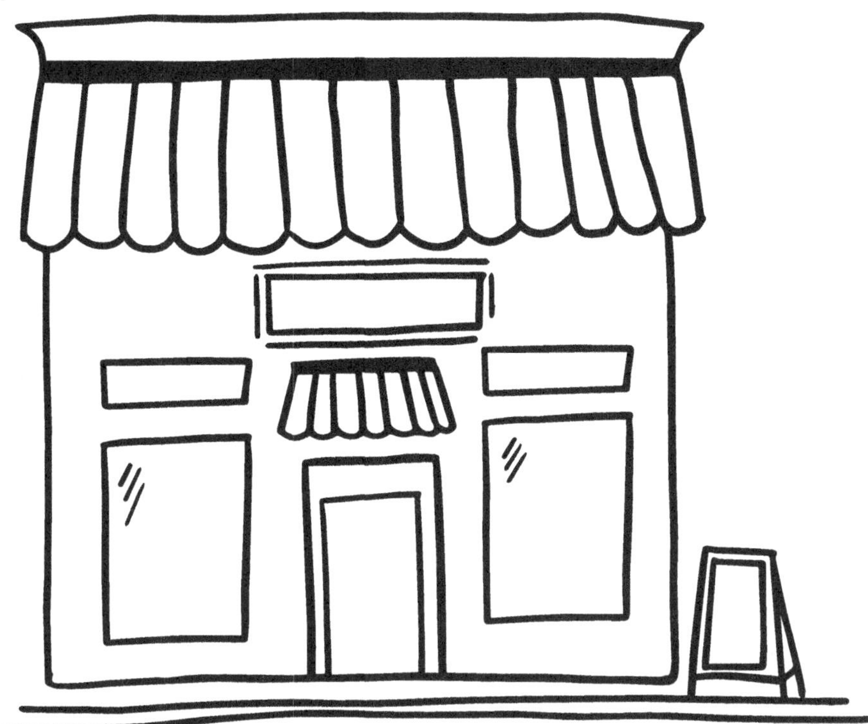

Draw your storefront below:

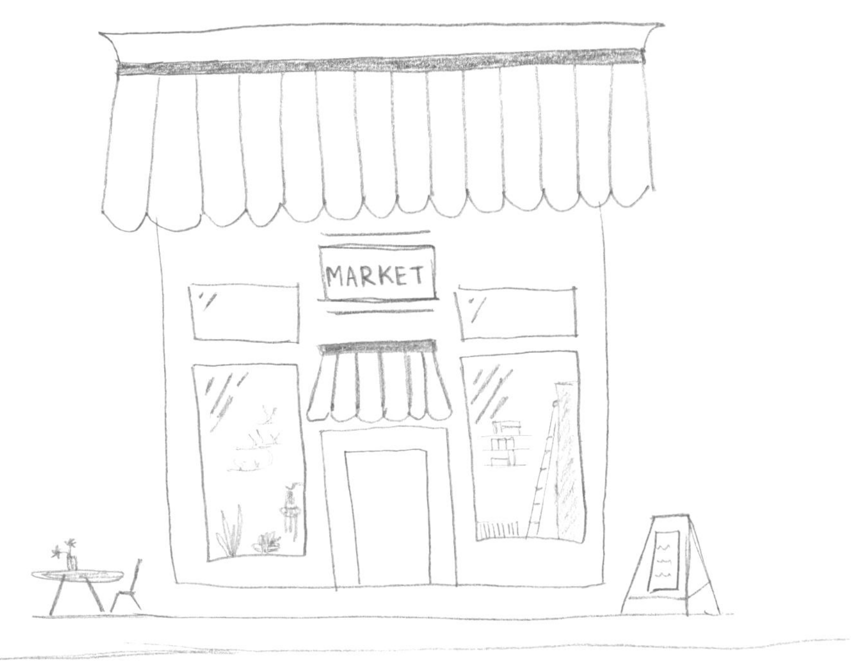

Let's draw a cactus

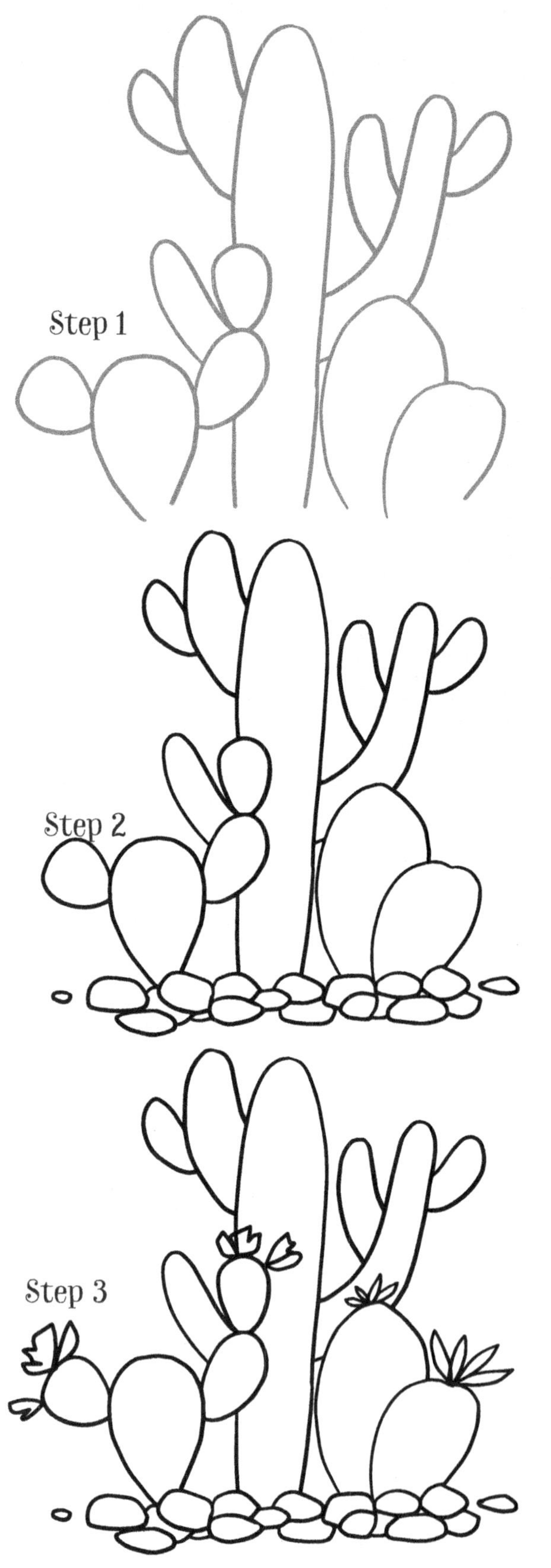

1. With a pencil draw a grouping of various cactus plants. Use different shapes and heights.

2. With a drawing pen trace over your pencil sketch. Adding rocks at the base of the plants.

3. With a pen add blooms on the tips of some of the cacti.

4. Finish the cactus plants by adding needles and line details.

Step 4

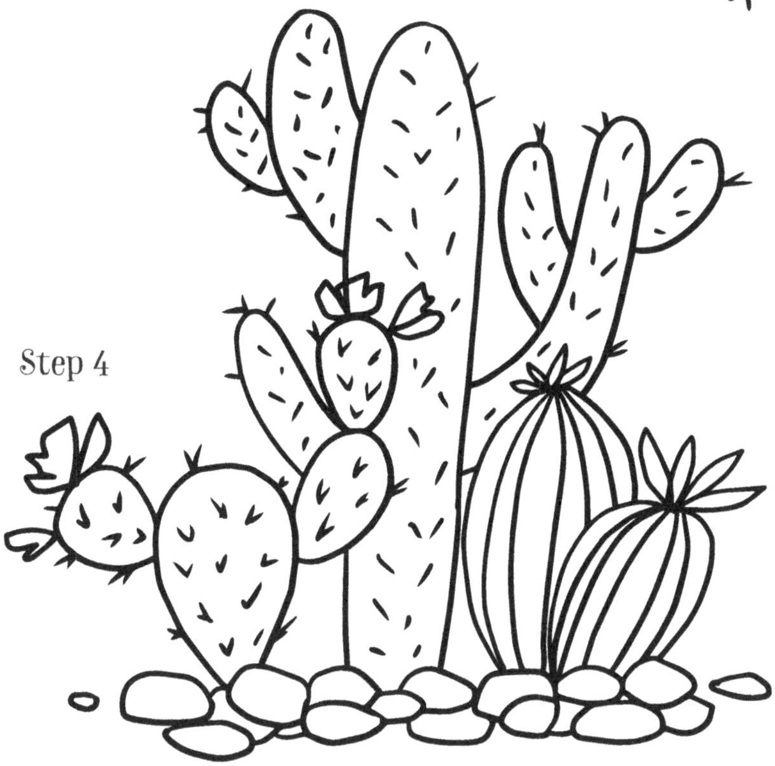

Draw your cactus below:

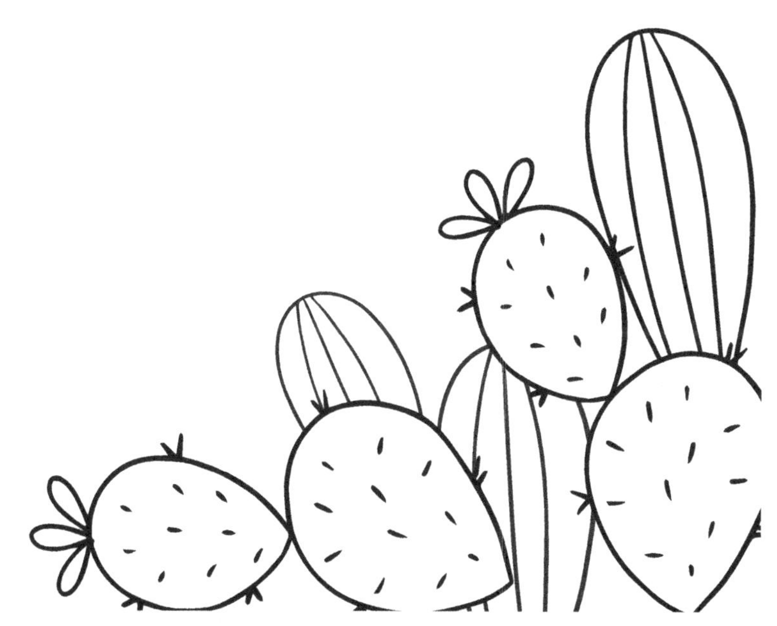

Let's draw

ice cream

Step 1

1. With a pencil draw a cherry on top of one scoop of ice cream.

Step 2

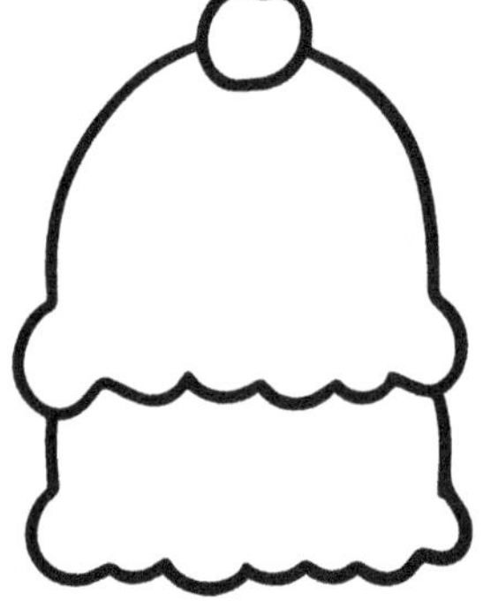

2. With a drawing pen trace over your pencil sketch. Add another scoop under your top scoop of ice cream.

Step 3

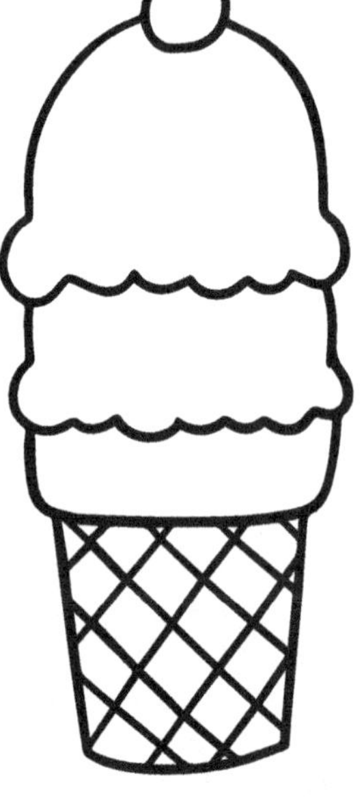

3. With a pen add the top of the ice cream cone and under that add the cone with line details.

4. Finish the ice cream by adding sprinkles on top.

Step 4

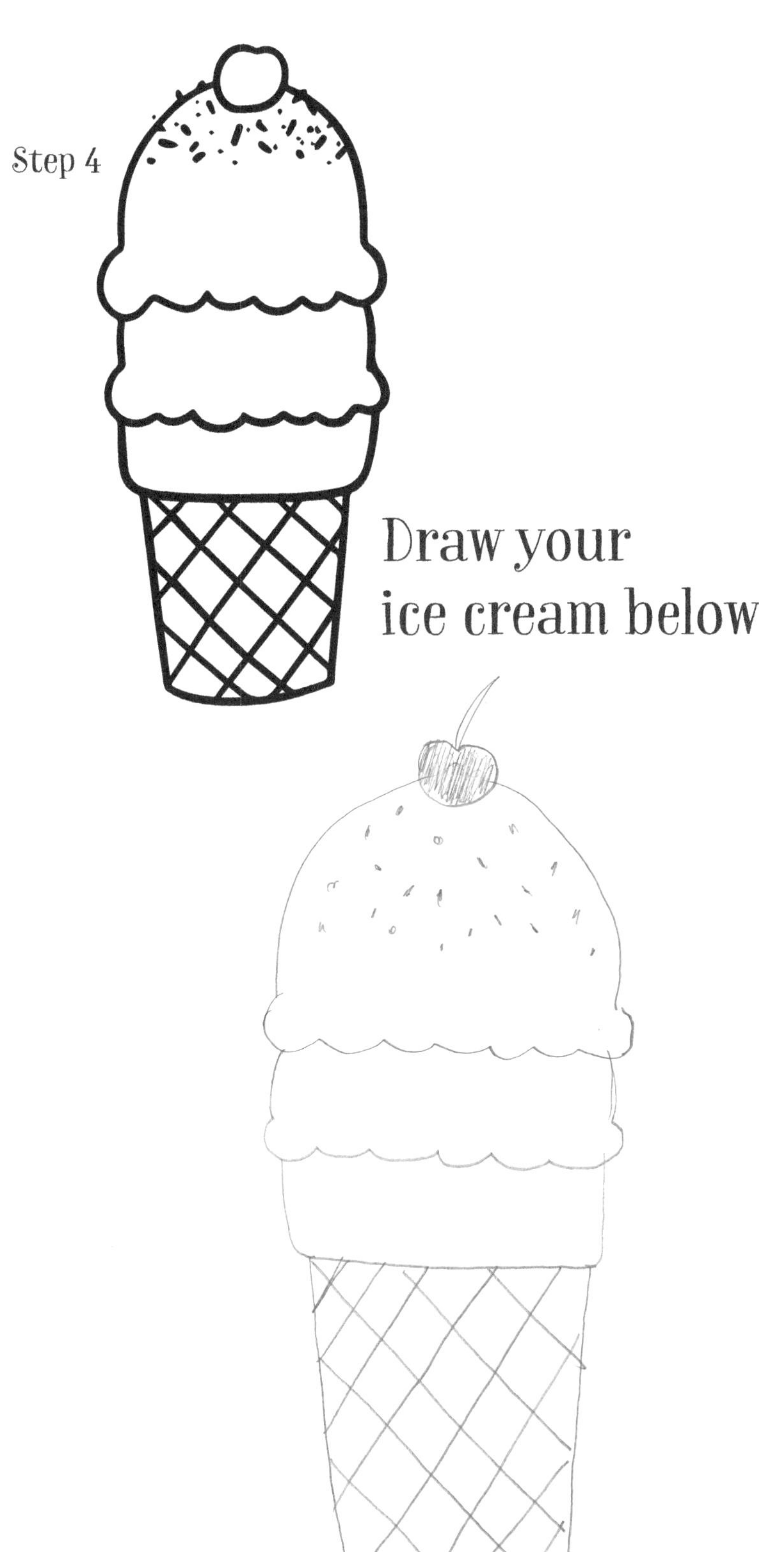

Draw your ice cream below:

Let's draw

a mixer:

Step 1

1. With a pencil draw a mixing bowl with an handle and a base.

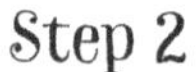

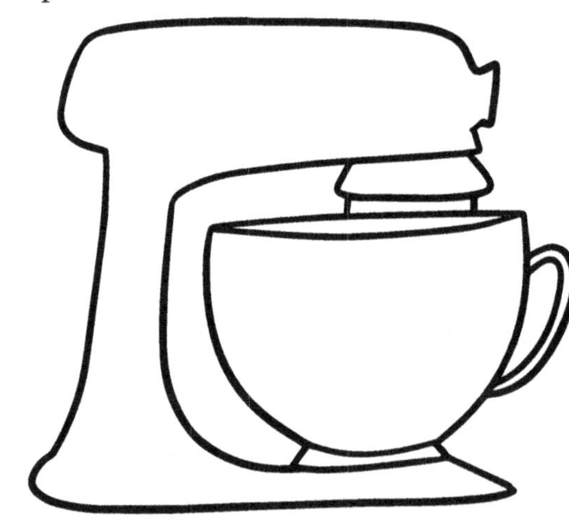

2. With a drawing pen trace over your pencil sketch. Add a stand mixer.

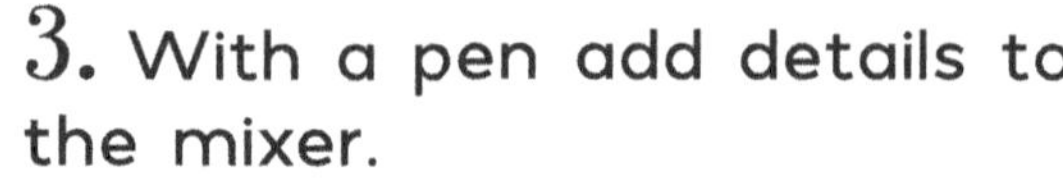

Step 3

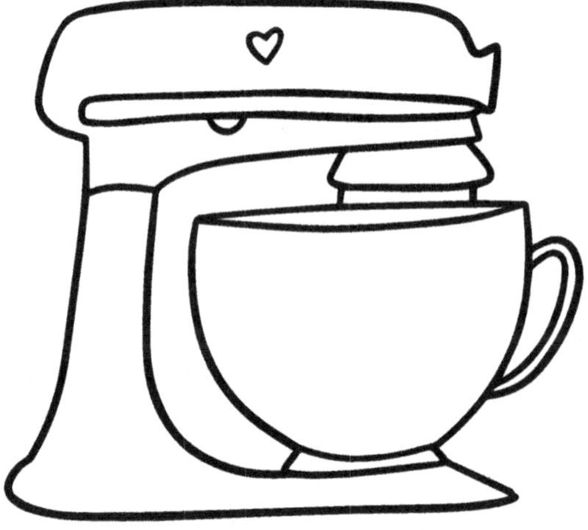

4. Finish the mixer by drawing a whisk, spatula, and measuring spoons.

Step 4

Draw your mixer below:

Let's draw
strawberries

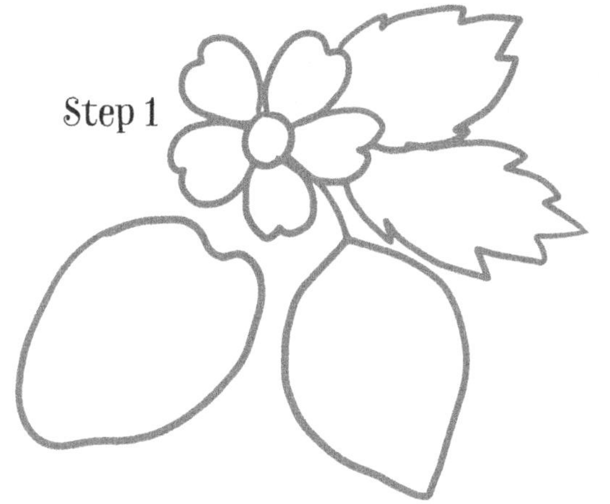

1. With a pencil draw a little strawberry flower and leaves. Add two strawberries below.

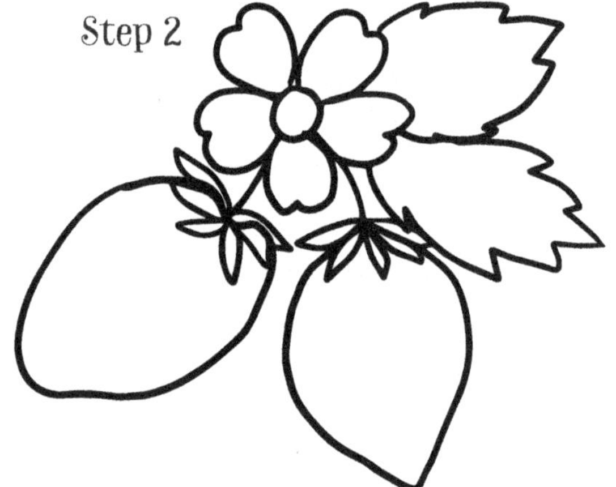

2. With a drawing pen trace over your pencil sketch. Add the little leafy green parts at the top of each strawberry.

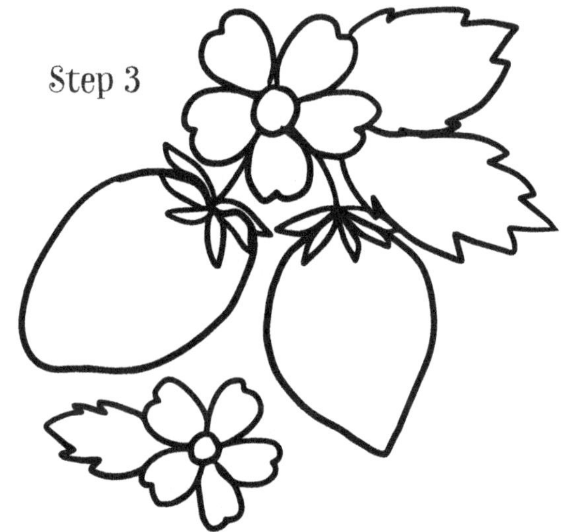

3. With a pen add another strawberry flower and leaf below the strawberries.

4. Finish the strawberries by adding seeds to each berry, and add line details on the leaves.

Step 4

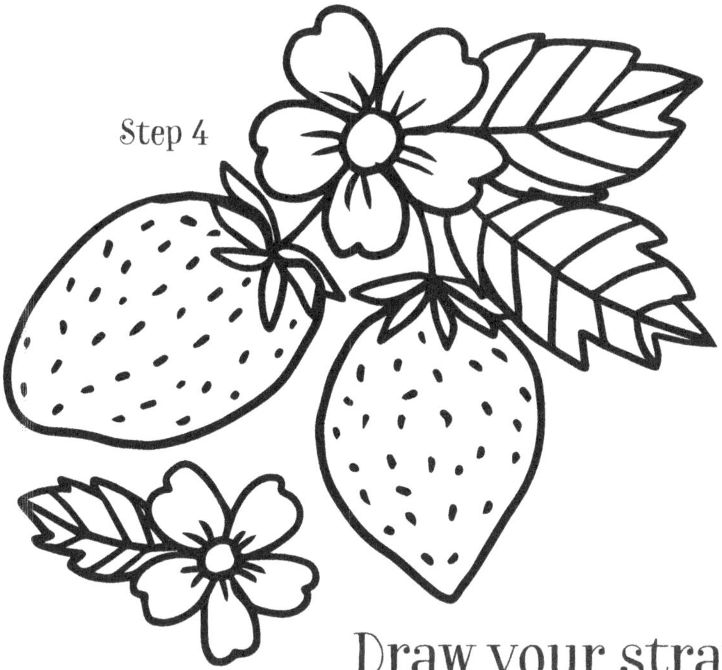

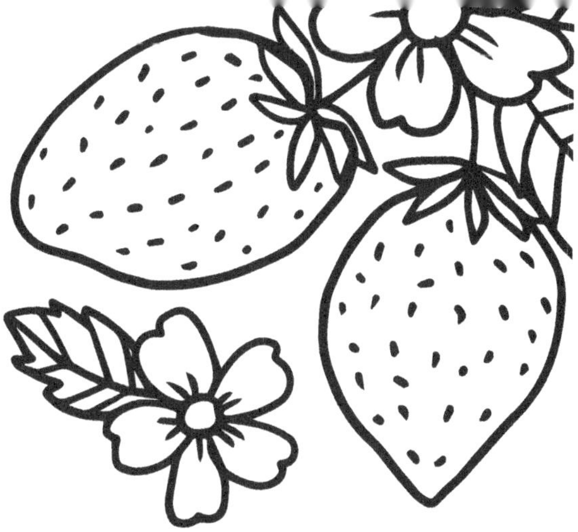

Draw your strawberries below:

Let's draw a mermaid:

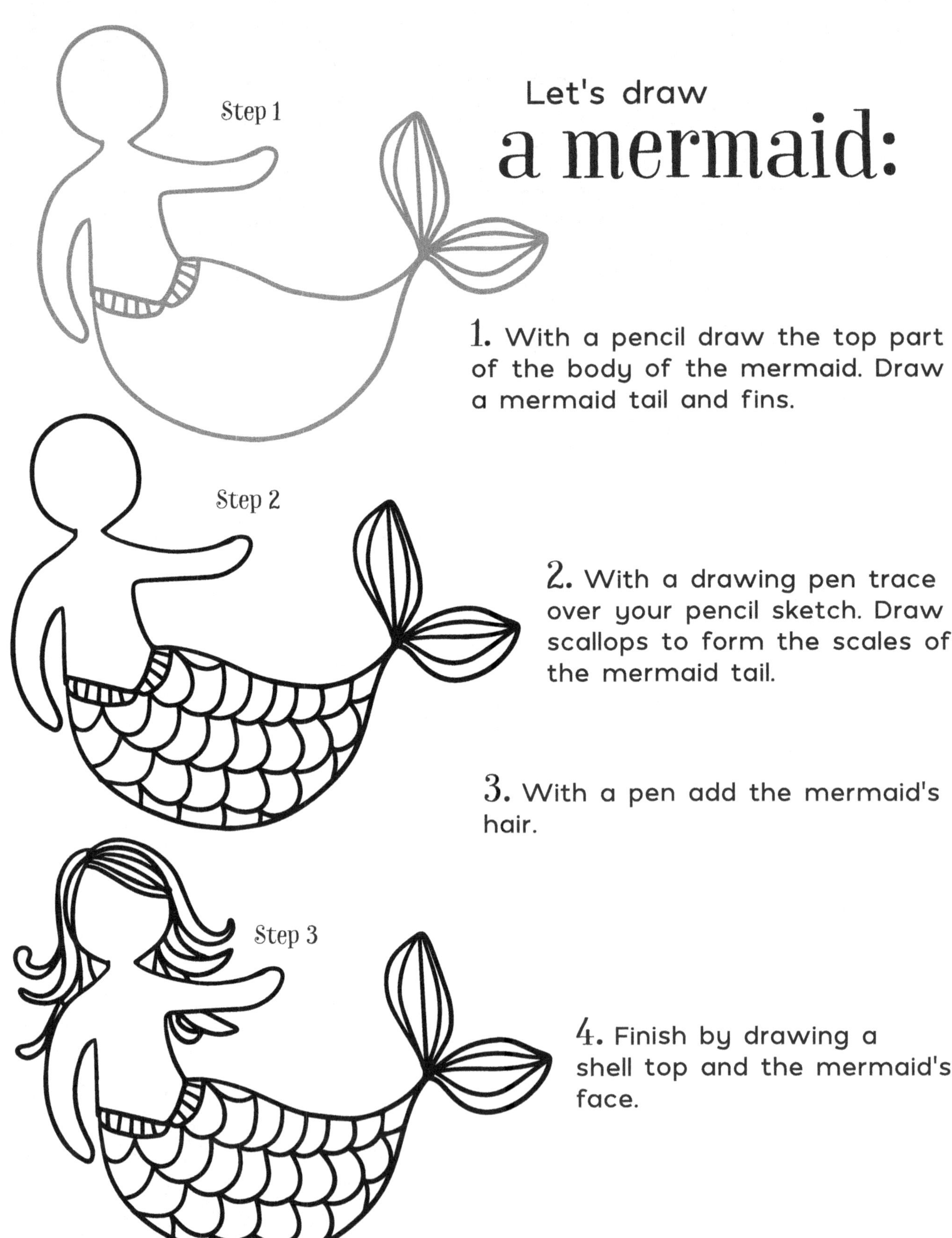

1. With a pencil draw the top part of the body of the mermaid. Draw a mermaid tail and fins.

2. With a drawing pen trace over your pencil sketch. Draw scallops to form the scales of the mermaid tail.

3. With a pen add the mermaid's hair.

4. Finish by drawing a shell top and the mermaid's face.

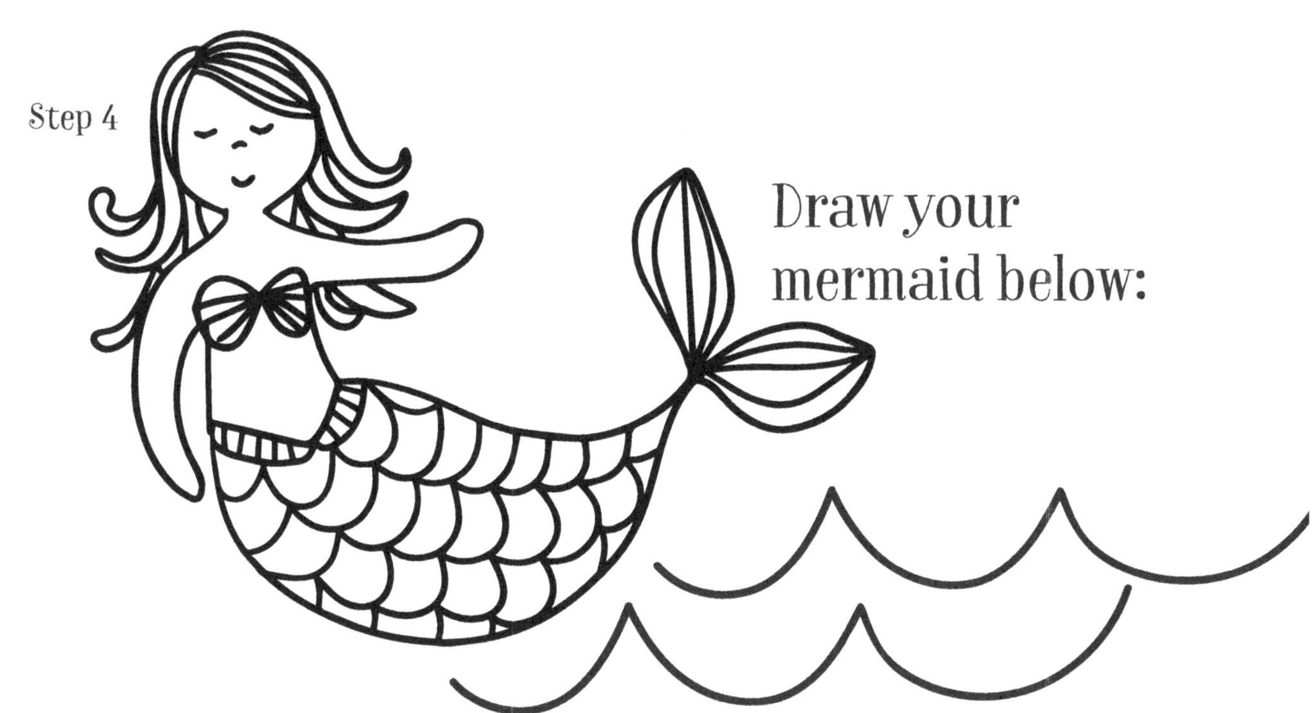

Draw your mermaid below:

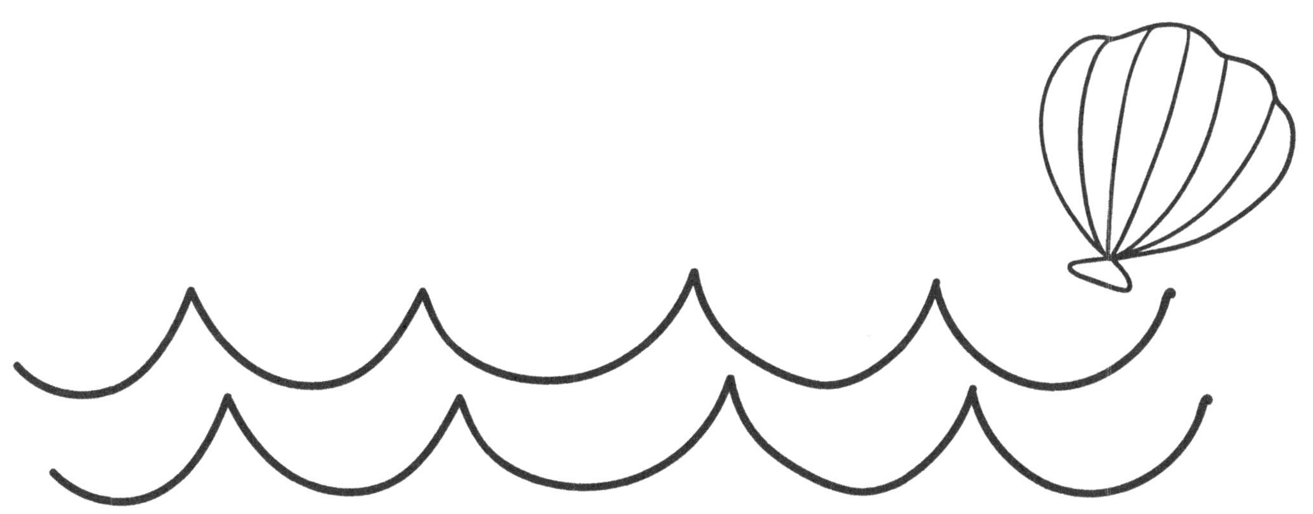

Let's draw

a swan:

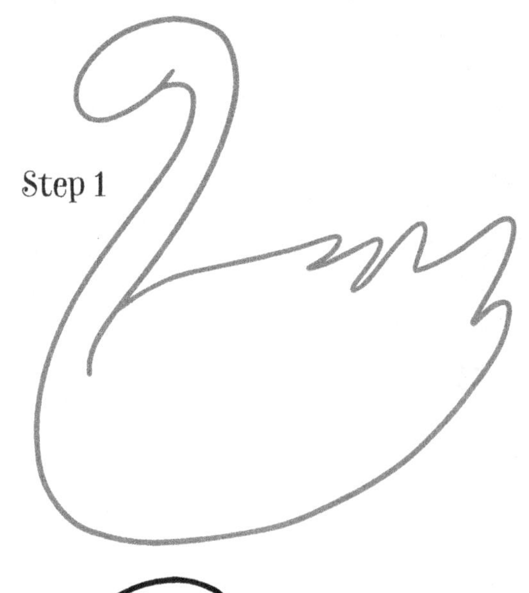

1. With a pencil draw the body of the swan including tail feathers.

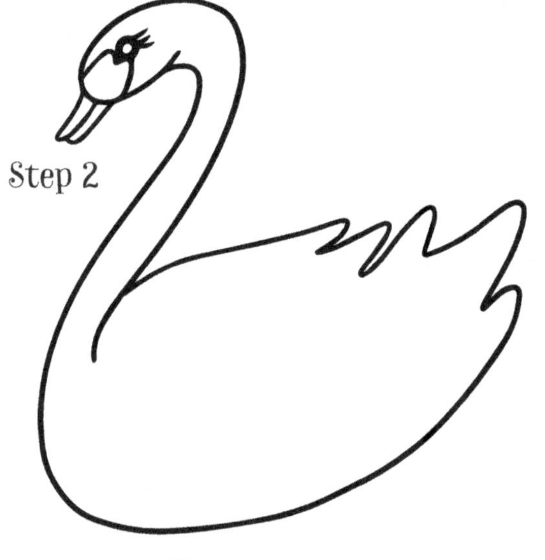

2. With a drawing pen trace over your pencil sketch. Add the swan's bill, the black part of its face, and its eye.

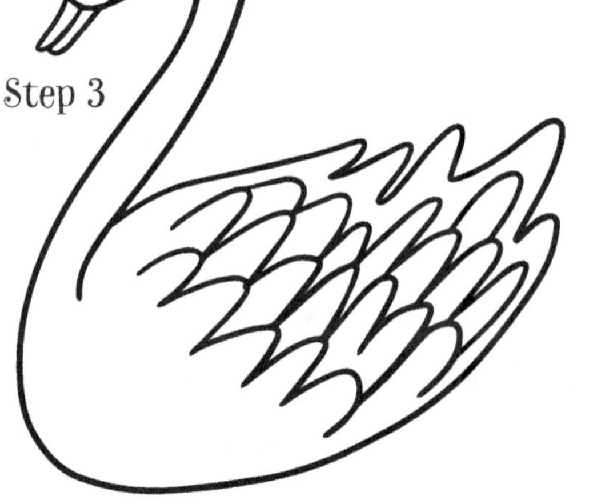

3. With a pen add layers of feathers to the swan from the chest up towards the tail.

4. Finish the swan by adding ripples of water under your drawing.

Step 4

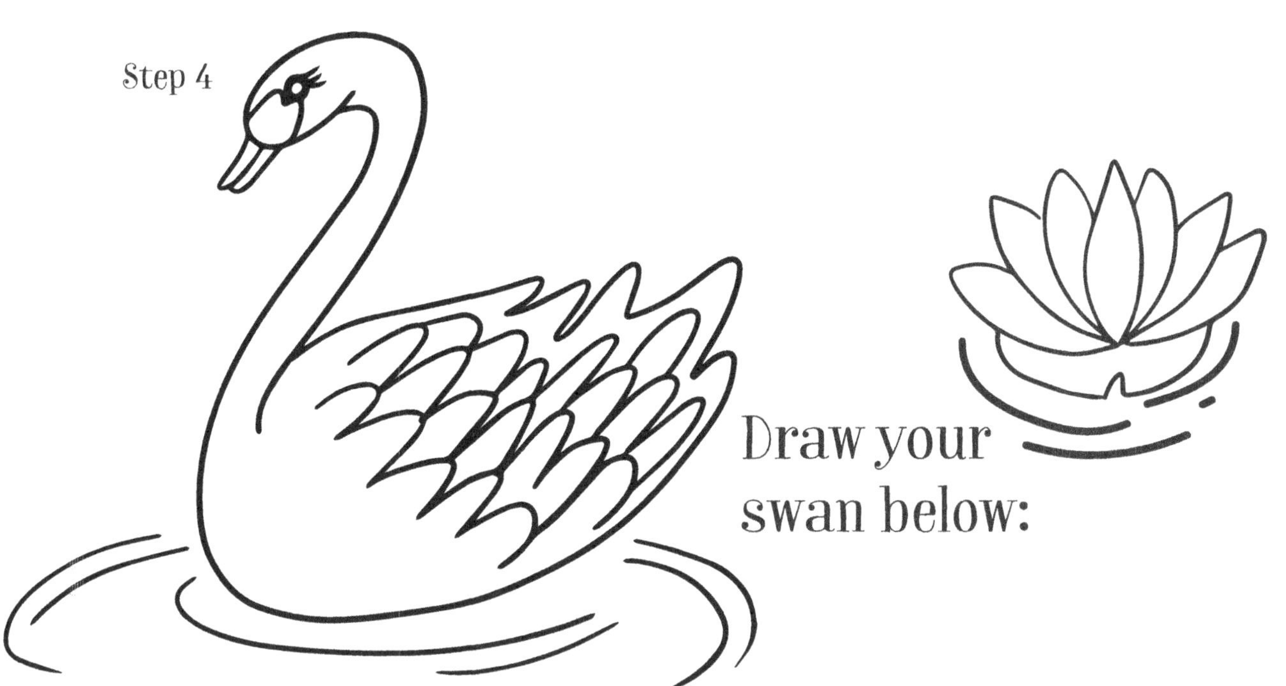

Draw your swan below:

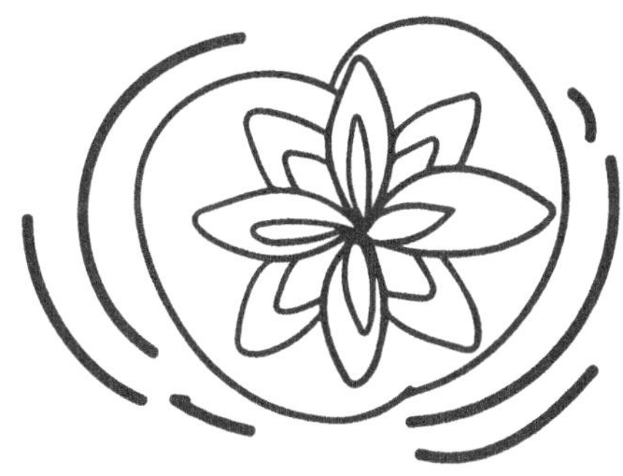

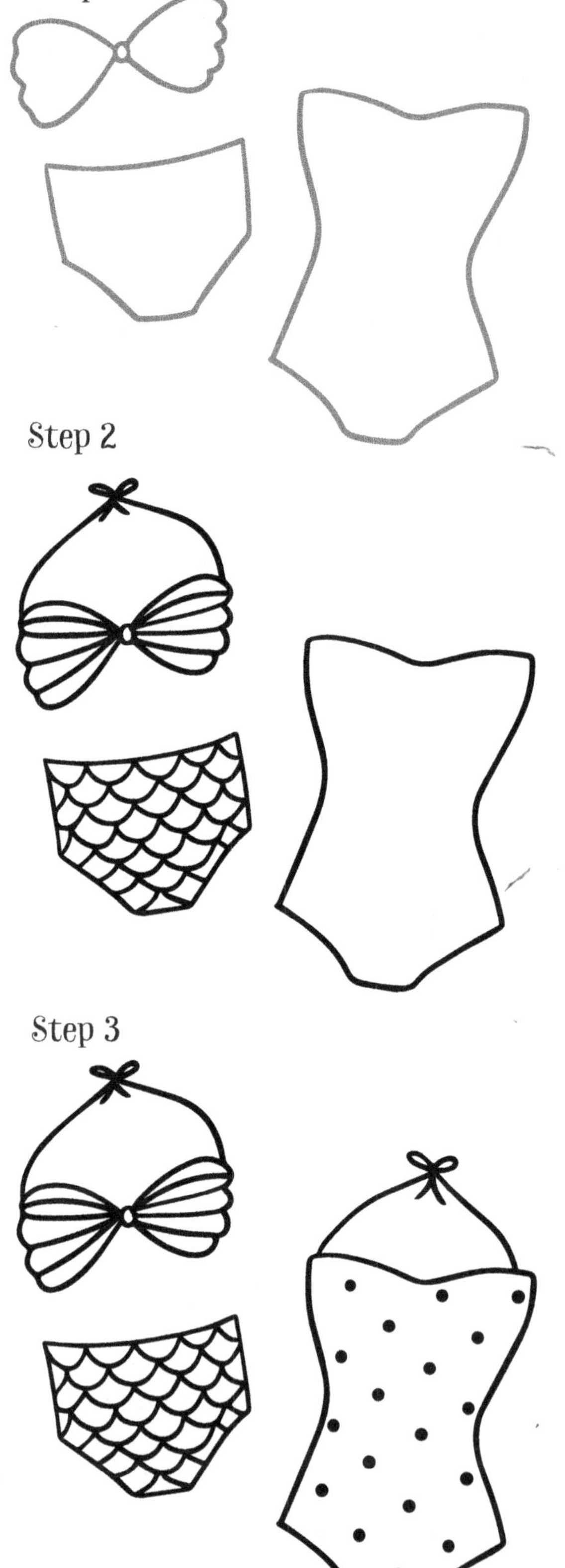

Let's draw

swimsuits:

1. With a pencil draw the outline of a two piece and a one piece swimsuit.

2. With a drawing pen trace over your pencil sketch. Add details to the two piece suit by drawing lines to look like seashells for the top and scallops for the bottom. Draw a string on the top.

3. With a pen add polka-dots to the one piece suit and a string on the top.

4. Finish by adding a pair of flip flops and sunglasses to the drawing.

Step 4

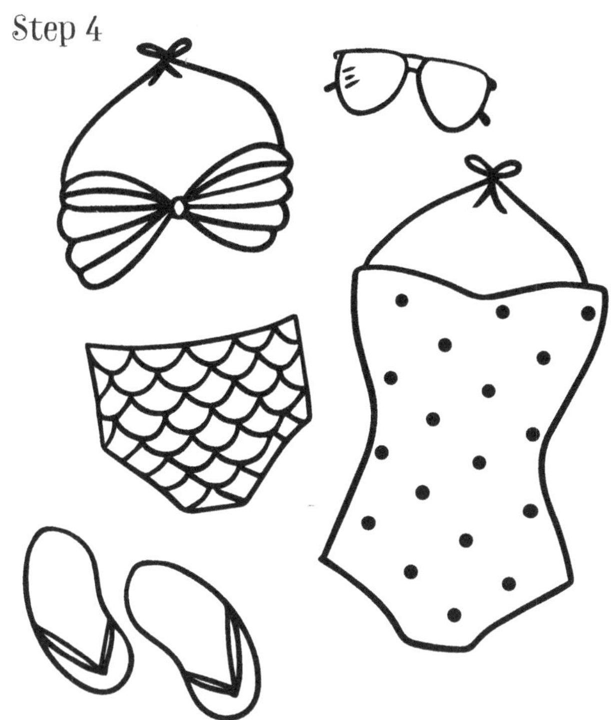

Draw your swimsuits below:

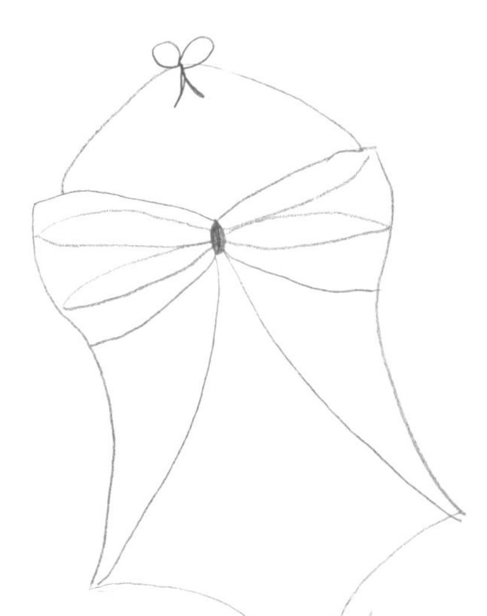

Let's draw

a unicorn

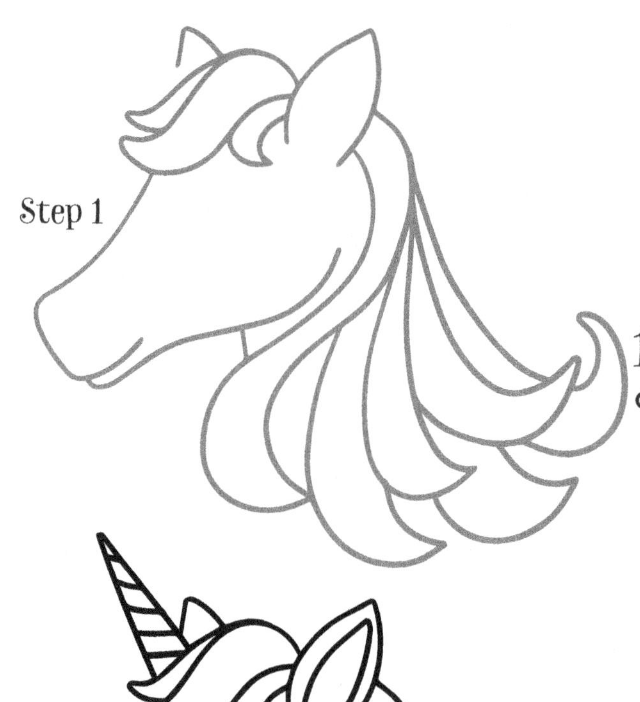

1. With a pencil draw the head of the unicorn with hair.

Step 2

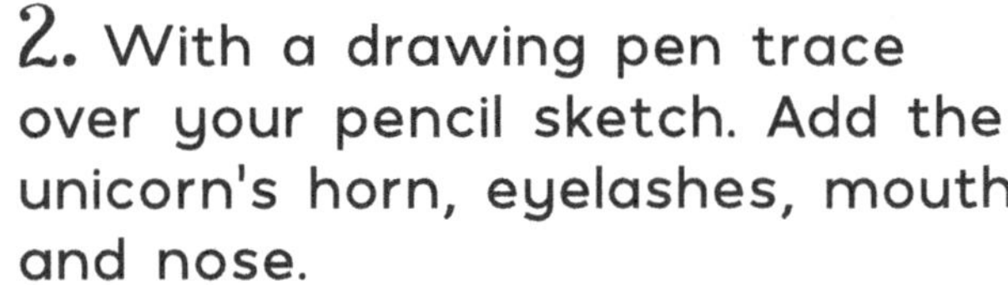

2. With a drawing pen trace over your pencil sketch. Add the unicorn's horn, eyelashes, mouth and nose.

3. With a pen add detailed lines in the unicorn's hair.

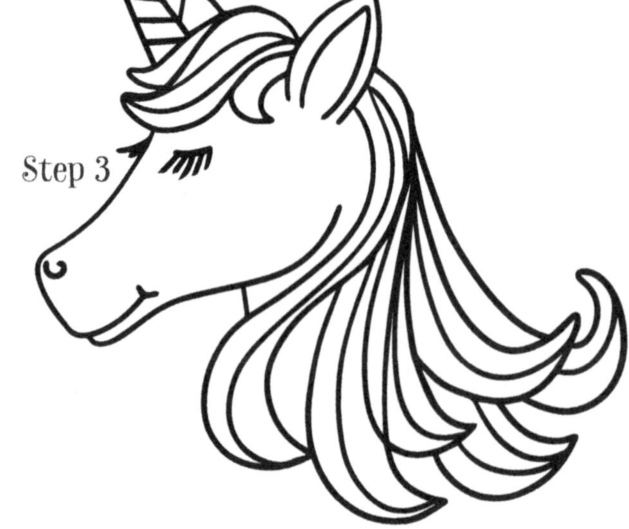

4. Finish the unicorn by adding star accents.

Step 4

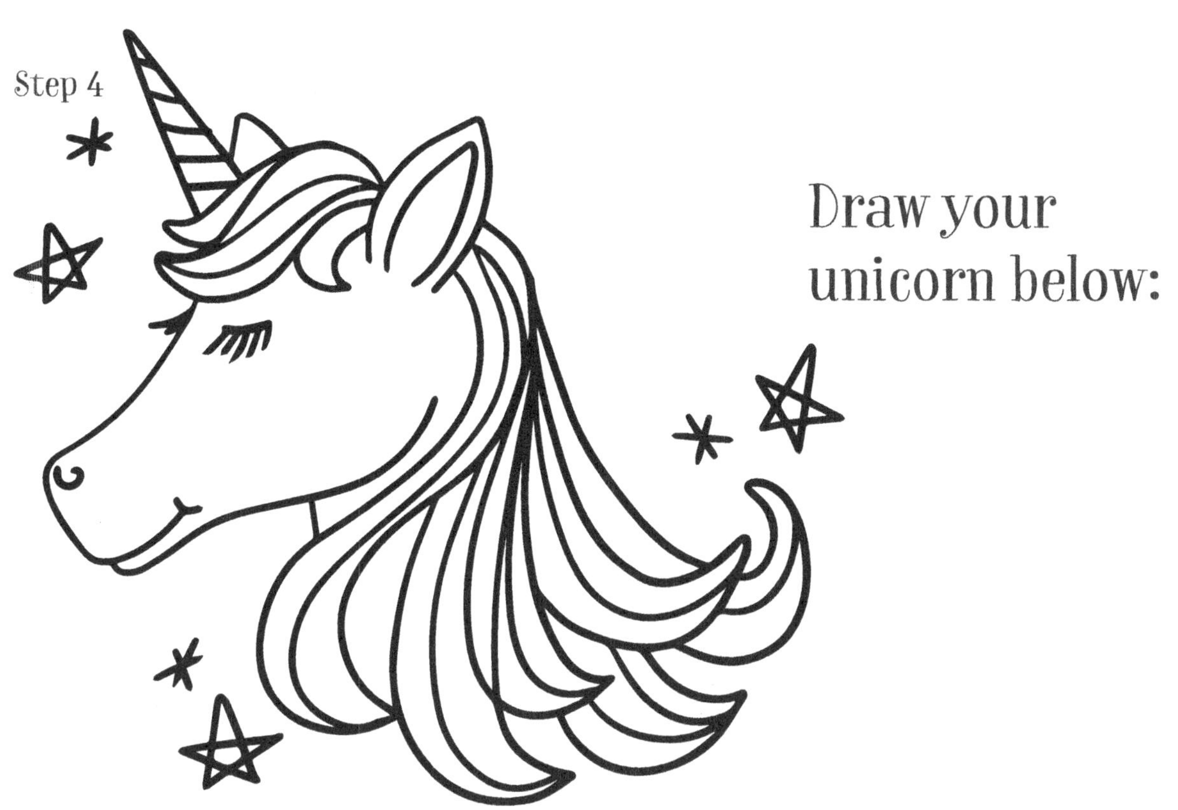

Draw your unicorn below:

Let's draw

poppies

Step 1

1. With a pencil draw two poppies. Draw one from a side angle and draw the second facing forward.

Step 2

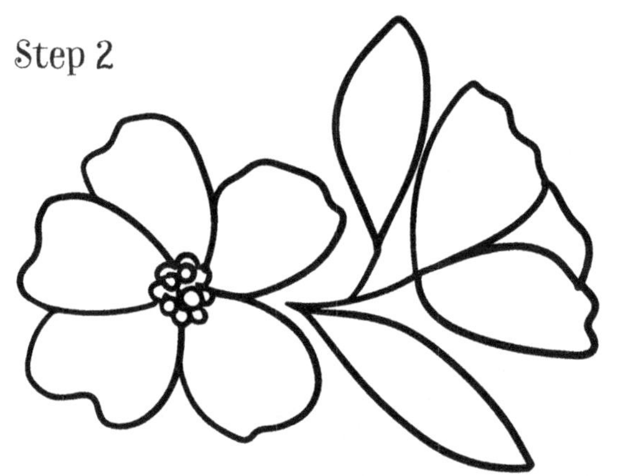

2. With a drawing pen trace over your pencil sketch. Add leaves on the stem of the side angled poppy.

3. With a pen add detailed lines on each petal of the poppies.

Step 3

4. Finish the poppies by adding line details on the leaves.

Step 4

Draw your poppies below:

Let's draw
succulents

Step 1

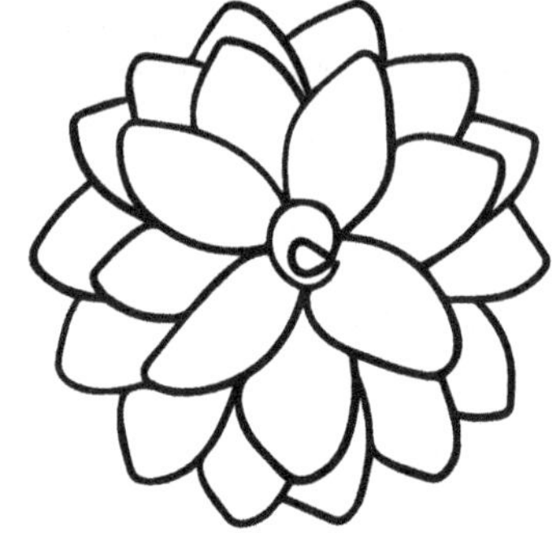

1. With a pencil draw a succulent, beginning with the center bud and working your way outward with layers.

Step 2

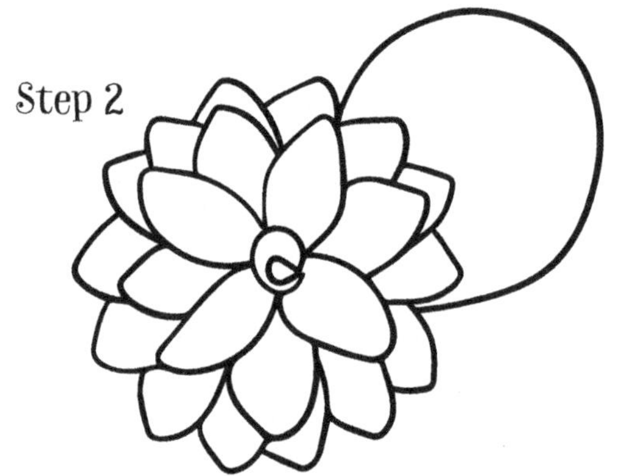

2. With a drawing pen trace over your pencil sketch. Add a curved line to the side to create a small cactus.

3. With a pen add spines and a flower to the cactus.

Step 3

4. Finish the succulents by adding an air plant to the bottom side and a little bud to the top side.

Step 4

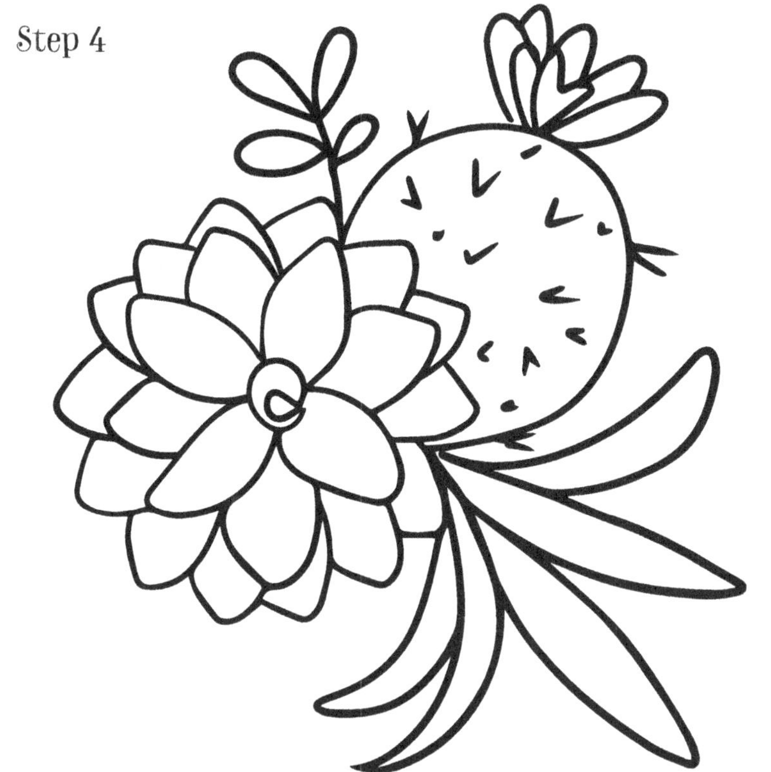

Draw your succulents below:

Let's draw tulips

Step 1

1. With a pencil draw one petal of the tulip.

Step 2

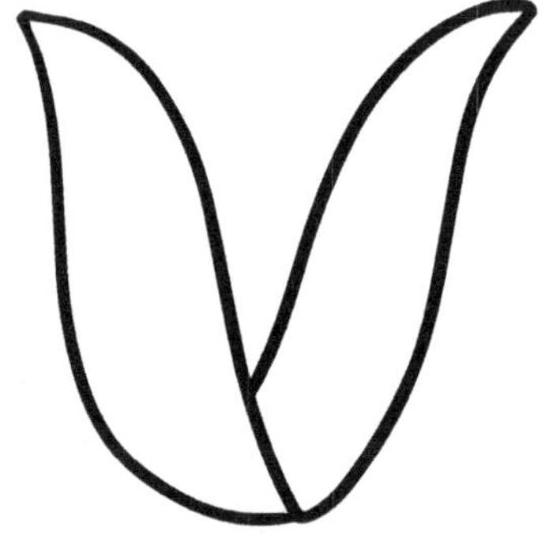

2. With a drawing pen trace over your pencil sketch. Add another petal to the tulip.

Step 3

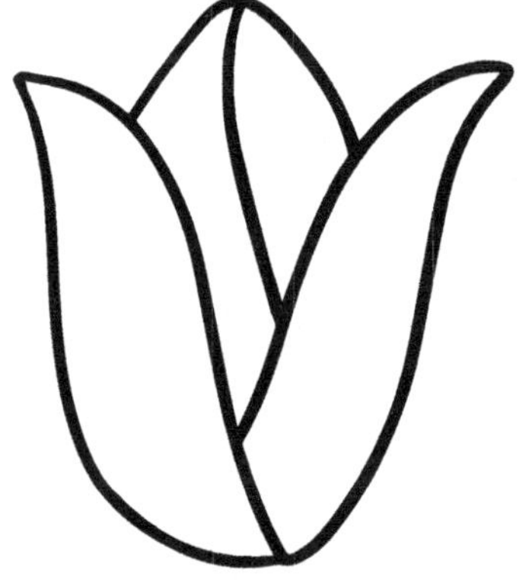

3. With a pen add petals to the middle of the tulip.

4. Finish the tulip by drawing a stem and two leaves on each side of the stem.

Step 4

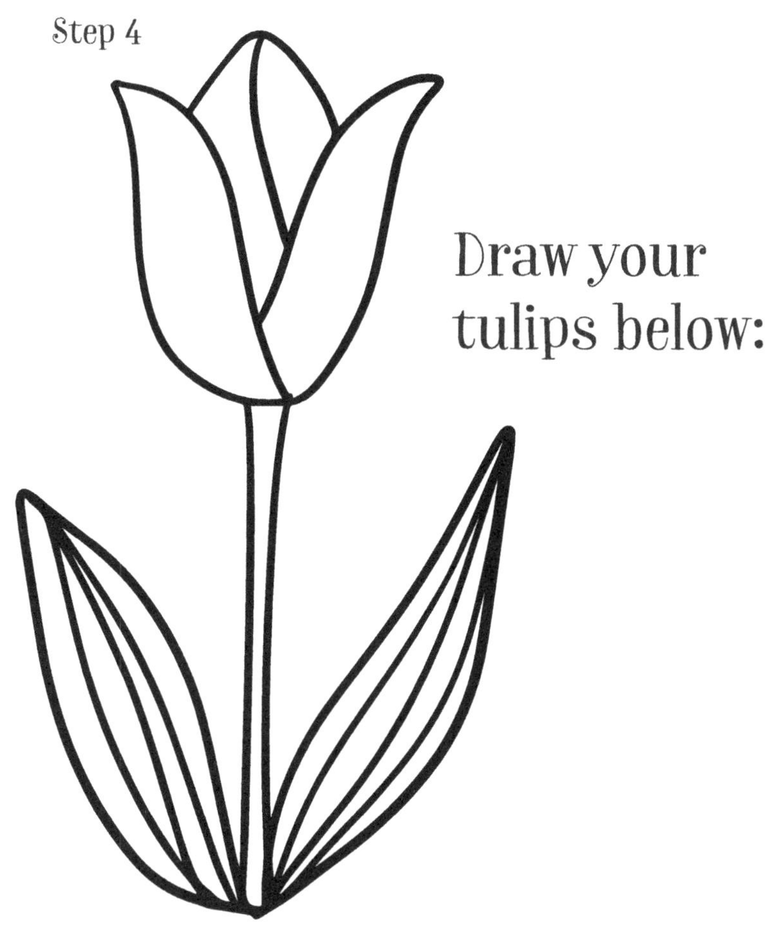

Draw your tulips below:

Step 1

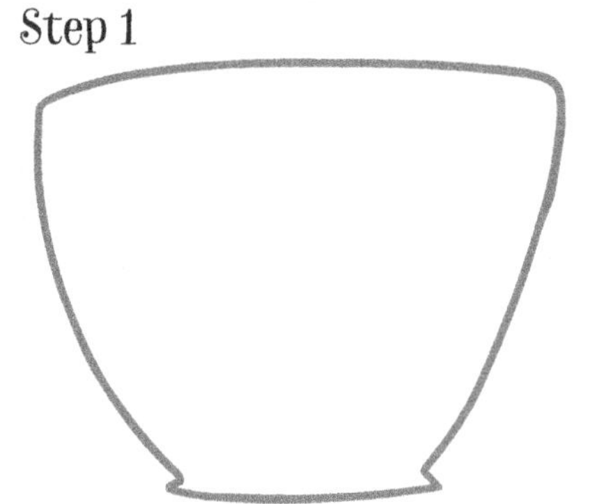

Let's draw a
cup of tea

1. With a pencil draw a tea cup.

Step 2

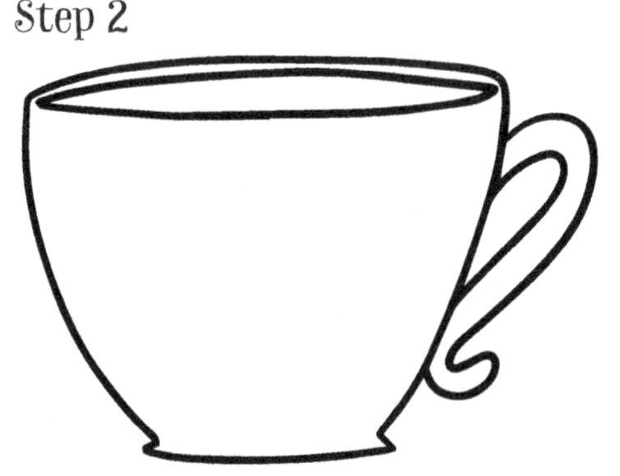

2. With a drawing pen trace over your pencil sketch. Add a rim at the top of the cup and a handle to the side.

3. With a pen add a saucer under the teacup.

Step 3

4. Finish the drawing by adding pretty details to the teacup.

Step 4

Draw your cup of tea below:

Let's draw a sunflower

Step 1

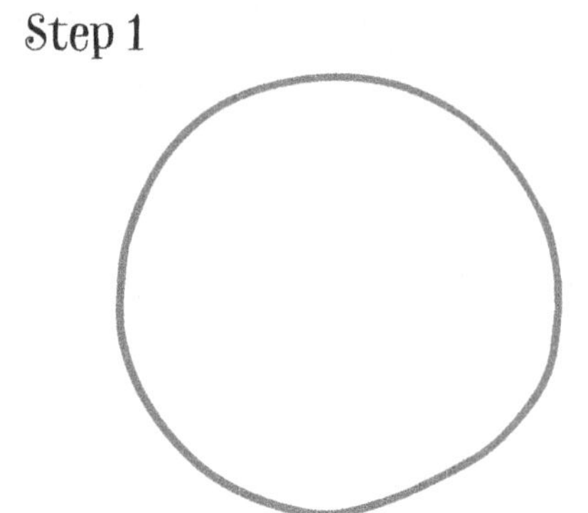

1. With a pencil draw a circle.

Step 2

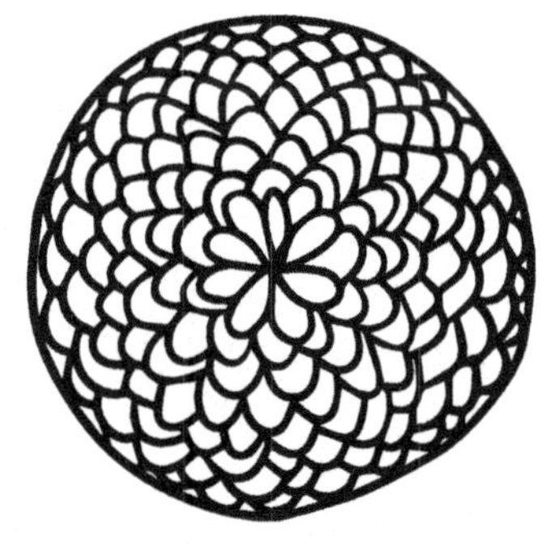

2. With a drawing pen trace over your pencil sketch. Begin adding disk florets starting in the center and adding layers all the way to the edge of the circle.

Step 3

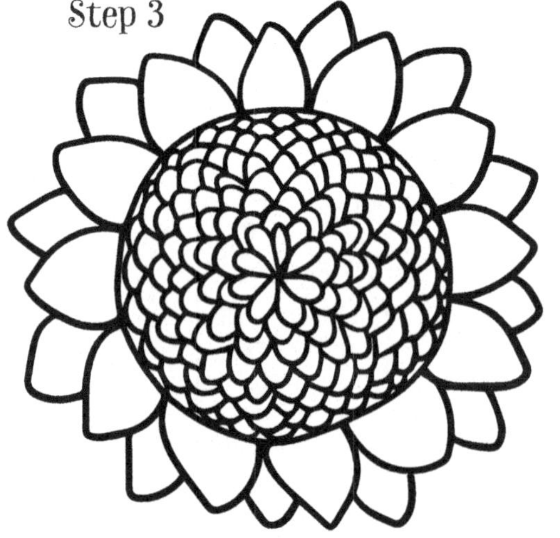

3. With a pen add petals all the way around the circle. Add a second layer of petals.

4. Finish the sunflower by adding accent lines to the center of each petal.

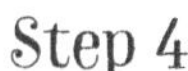

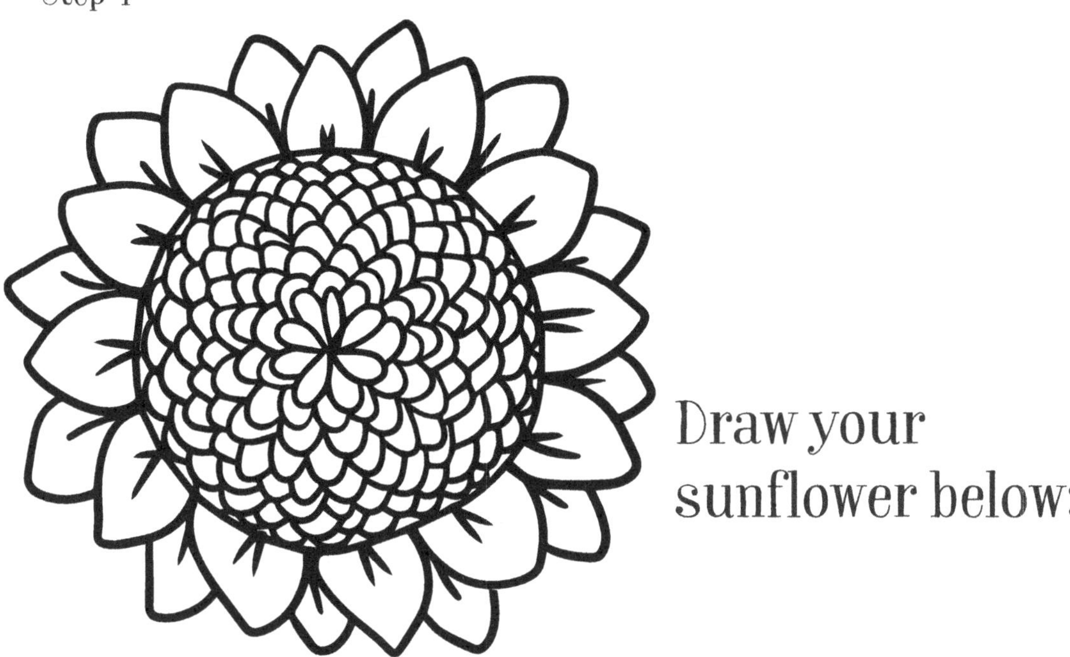

Draw your sunflower below:

Let's draw a

flower bouquet

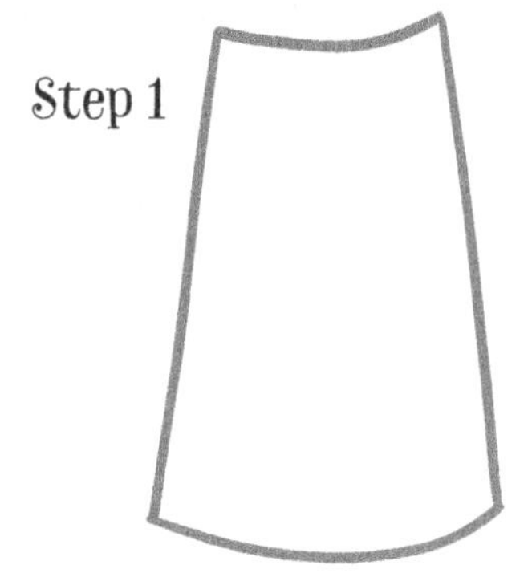

1. With a pencil draw a vase.

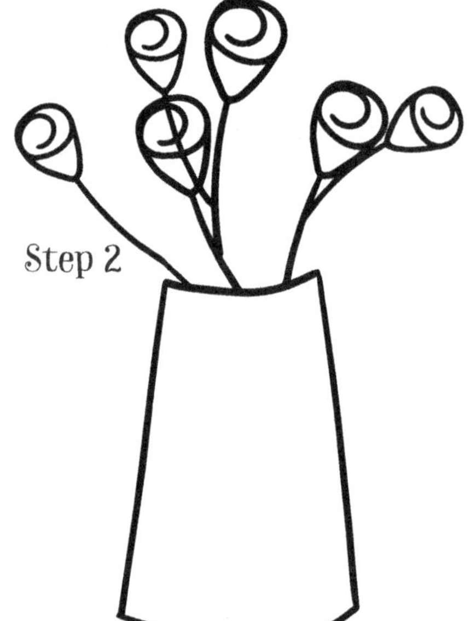

2. With a drawing pen trace over your pencil sketch. Add flowers to the vase.

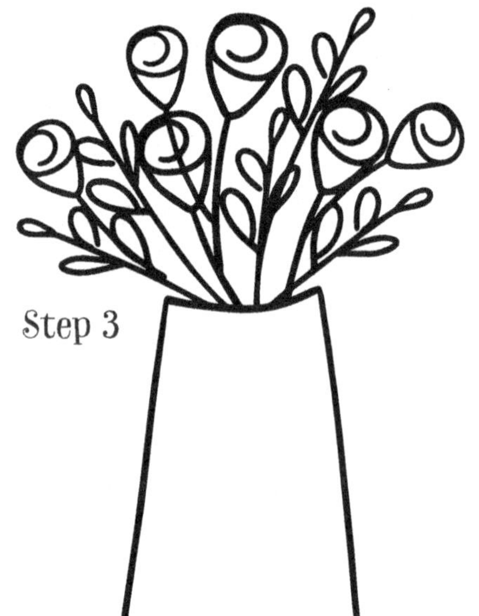

3. With a pen sprigs of of greenery between each flower.

4. Finish the bouquet of flowers by drawing details to the vase.

Step 4

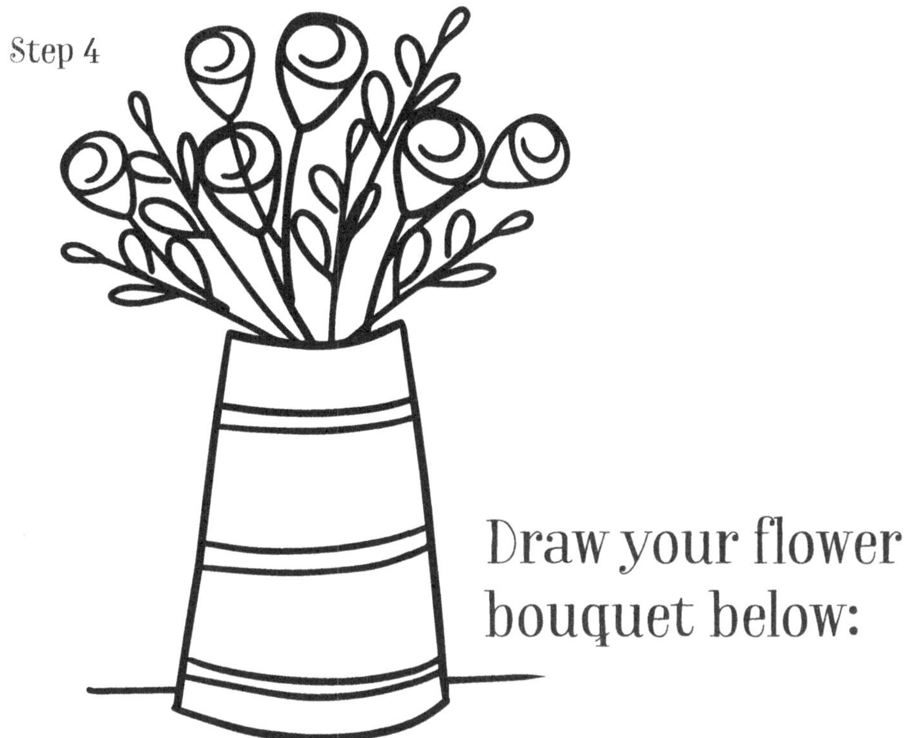

Draw your flower bouquet below:

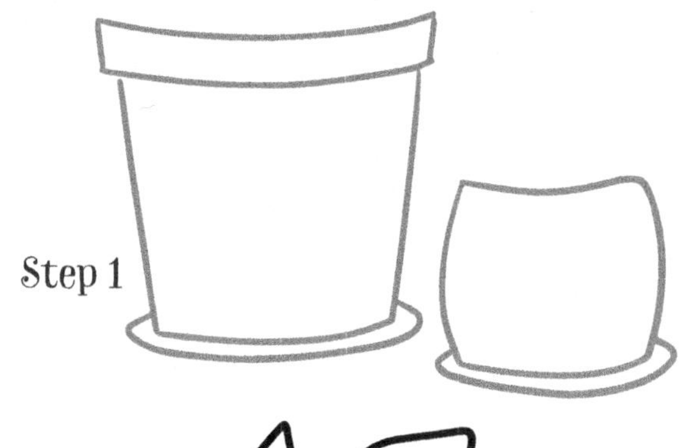

Let's draw
house plants

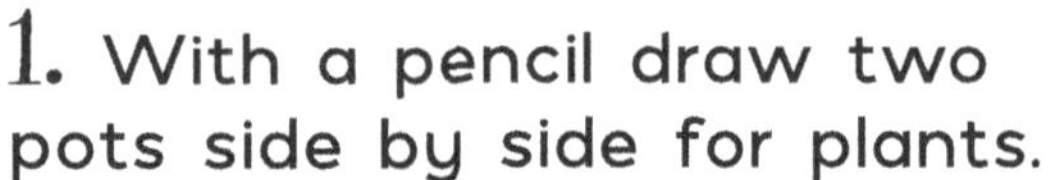
1. With a pencil draw two pots side by side for plants.

Step 2

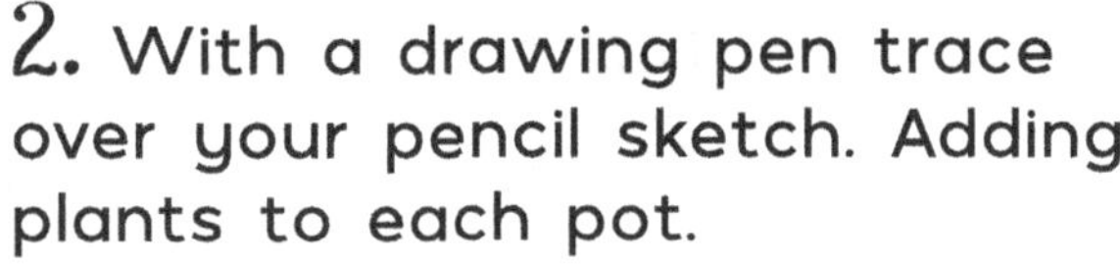
2. With a drawing pen trace over your pencil sketch. Adding plants to each pot.

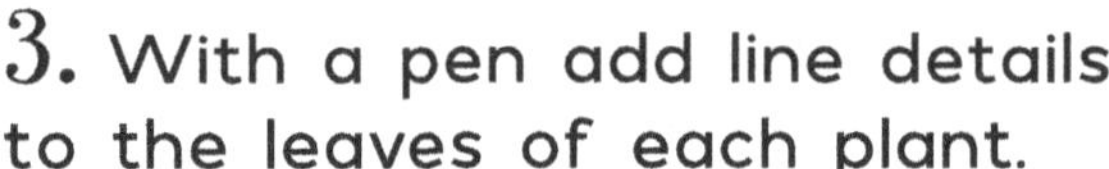
3. With a pen add line details to the leaves of each plant.

Step 3

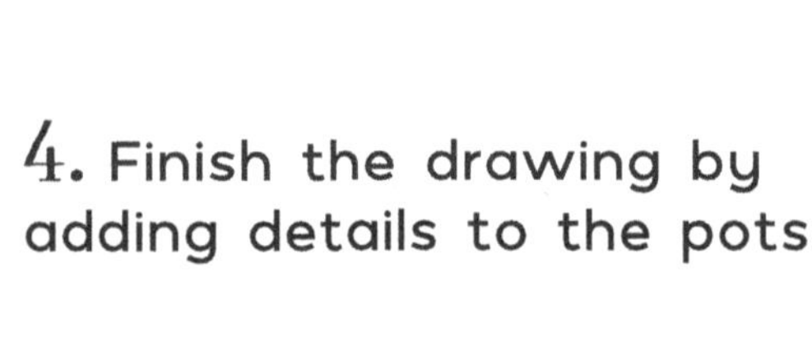
4. Finish the drawing by adding details to the pots.

Step 4

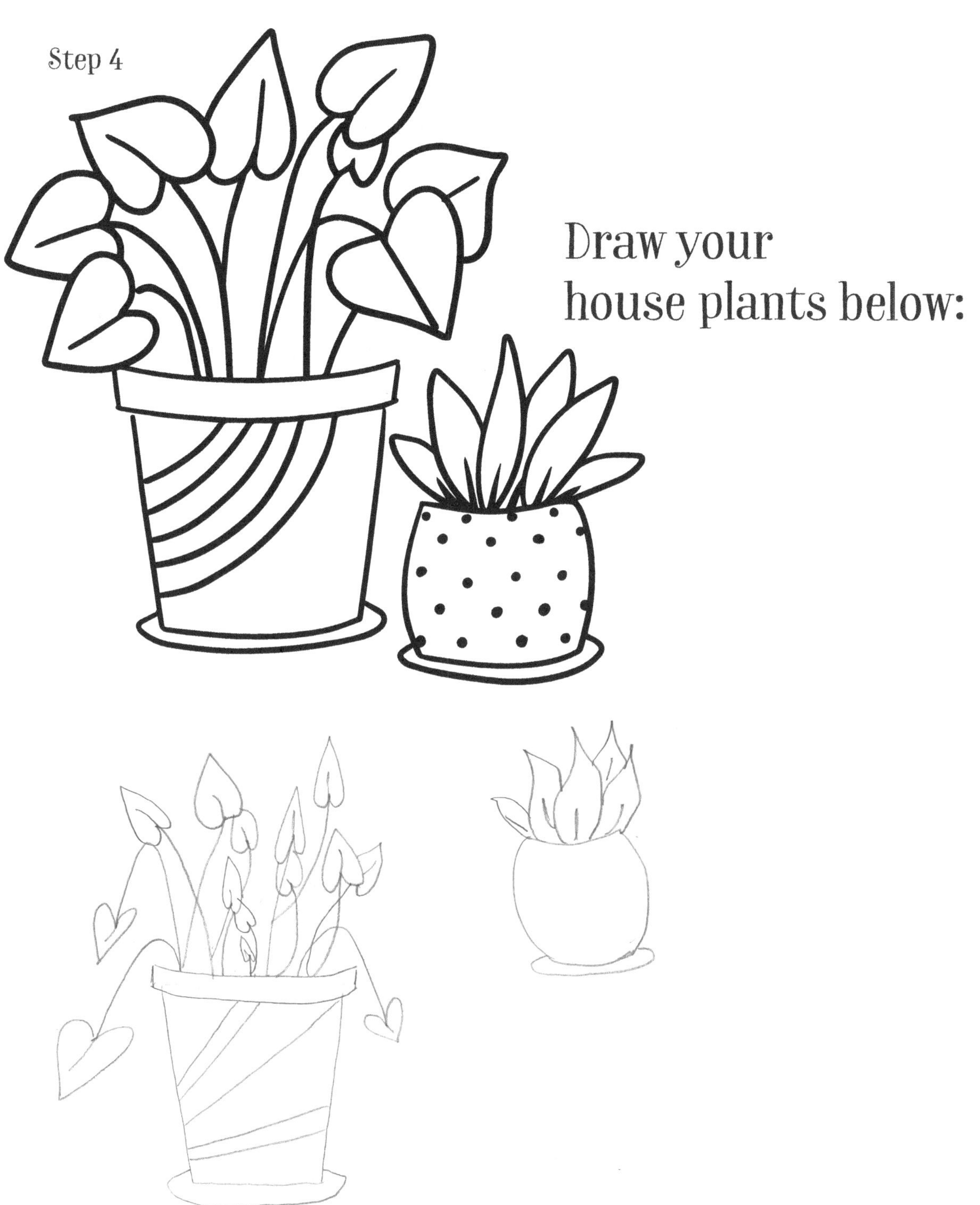

Draw your house plants below:

Let's draw a cupcake

Step 1

1. With a pencil draw the bottom portion of the cupcake.

Step 2

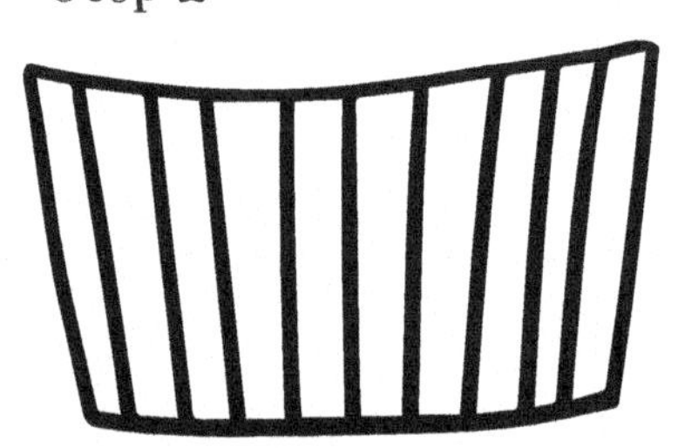

2. With a drawing pen trace over your pencil sketch. Add line details to the cupcake.

Step 3

3. With a pen add the top part of the cupcake with sprinkles.

4. Finish the drawing by adding a cute stand under the cupcake.

Step 4

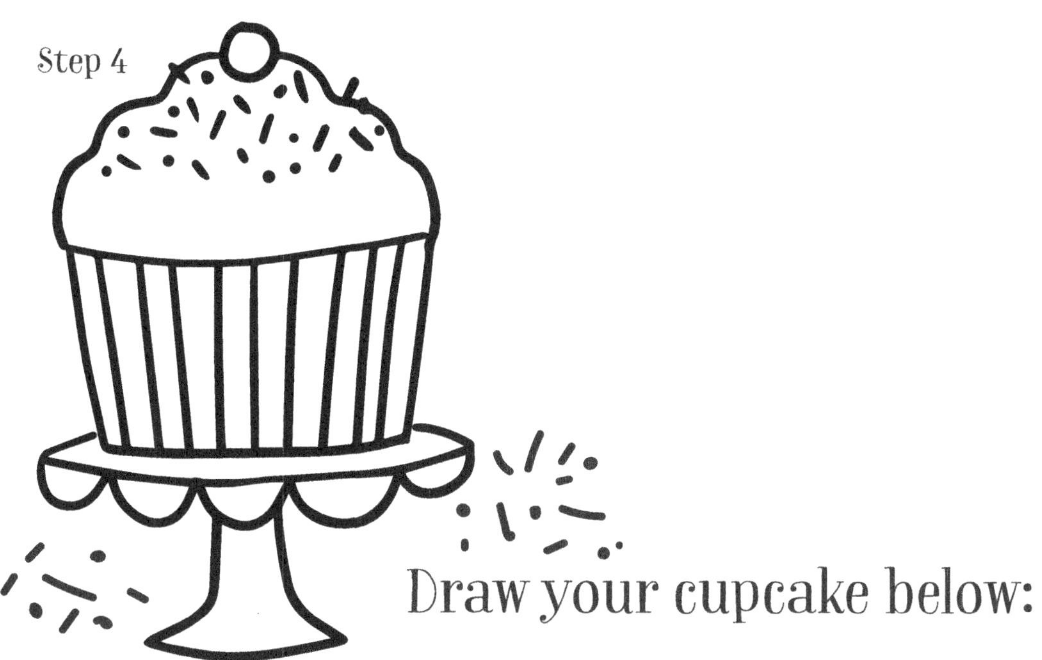

Draw your cupcake below:

Step 1

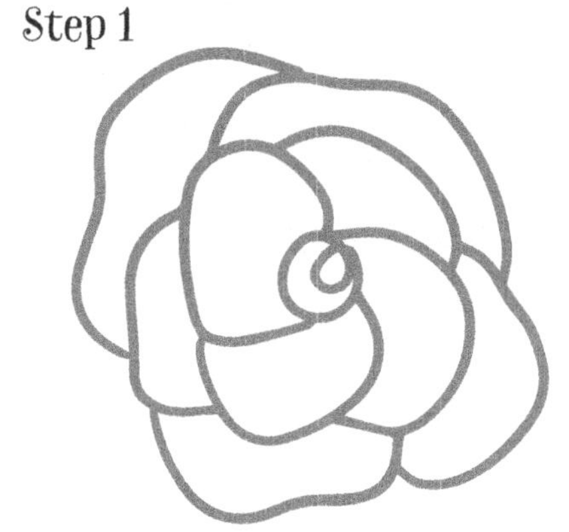

Let's draw a

rose

1. With a pencil draw a rose, starting from the center and adding petals in layers.

Step 2

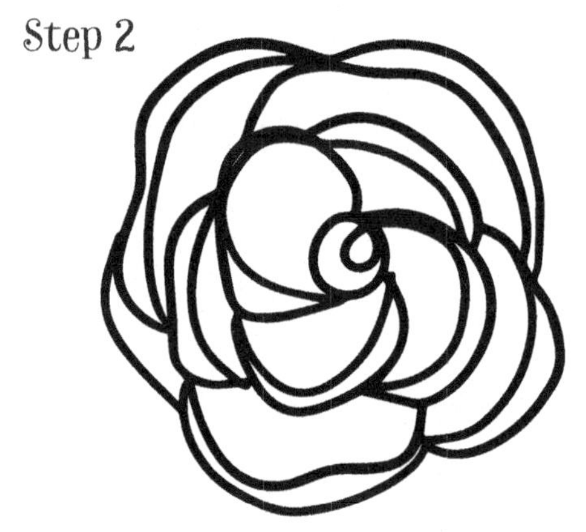

2. With a drawing pen trace over your pencil sketch. Add lines to the edge of each petal.

Step 3

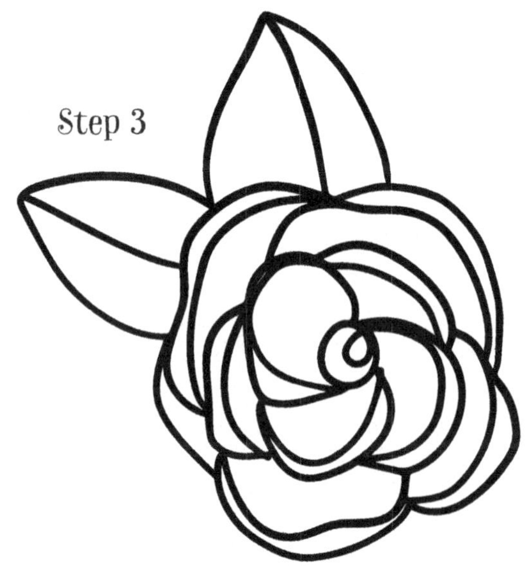

3. With a pen leaves to the side of the rose.

4. Finish the drawing by adding rosebuds on each side of the main flower.

Step 4

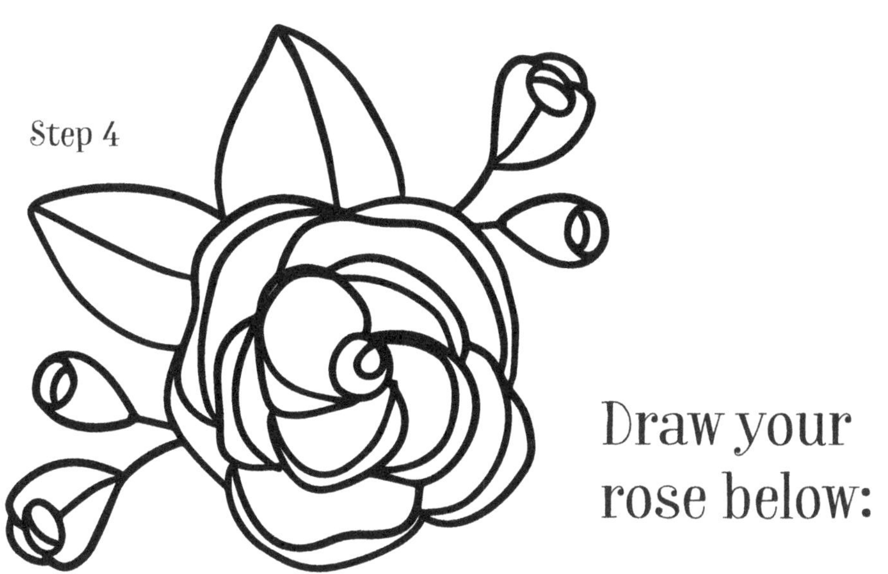

Draw your rose below:

Step 1

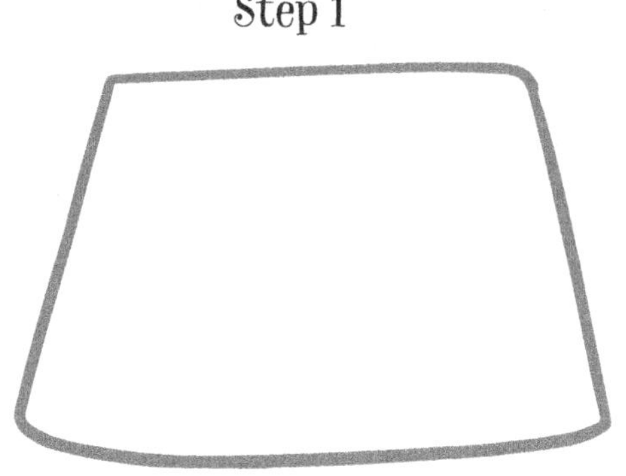

Let's draw a typewriter

1. With a pencil draw a trapezoid shape for the base of the typewriter.

Step 2

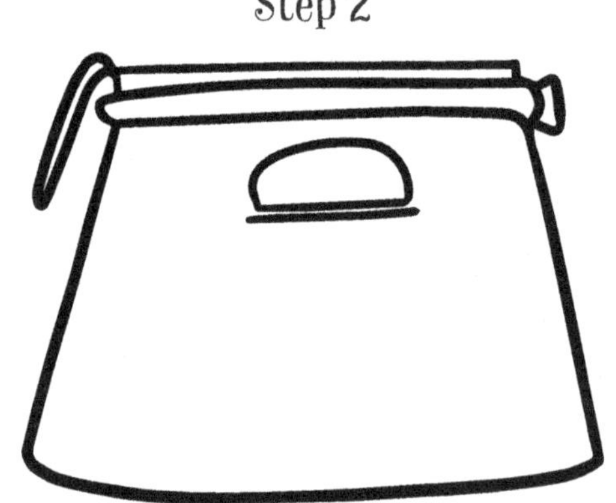

2. With a drawing pen trace over your pencil sketch. Add the lever and paper roller along with a section for the typebars.

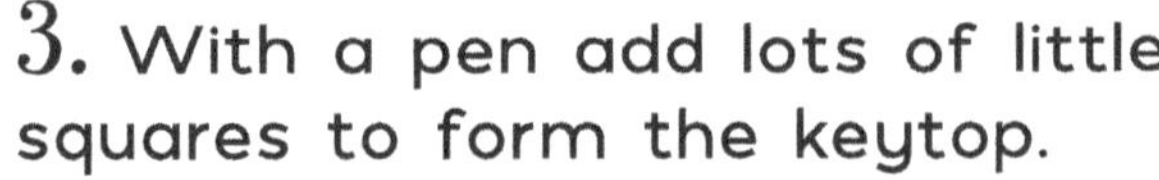

3. With a pen add lots of little squares to form the keytop.

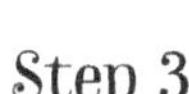

Step 3

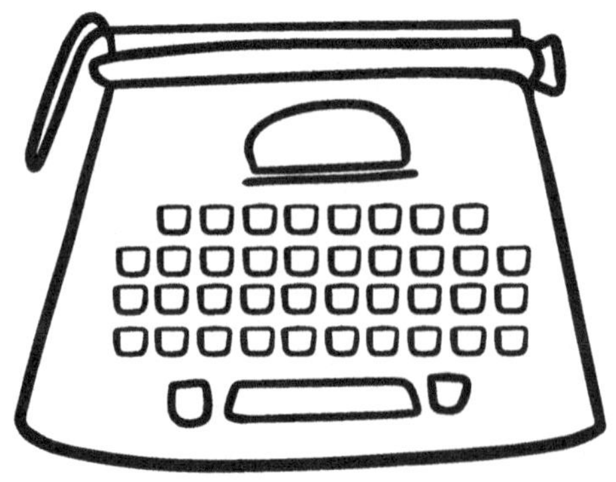

4. Finish the typewriter by drawing a piece of paper coming out of the top portion.

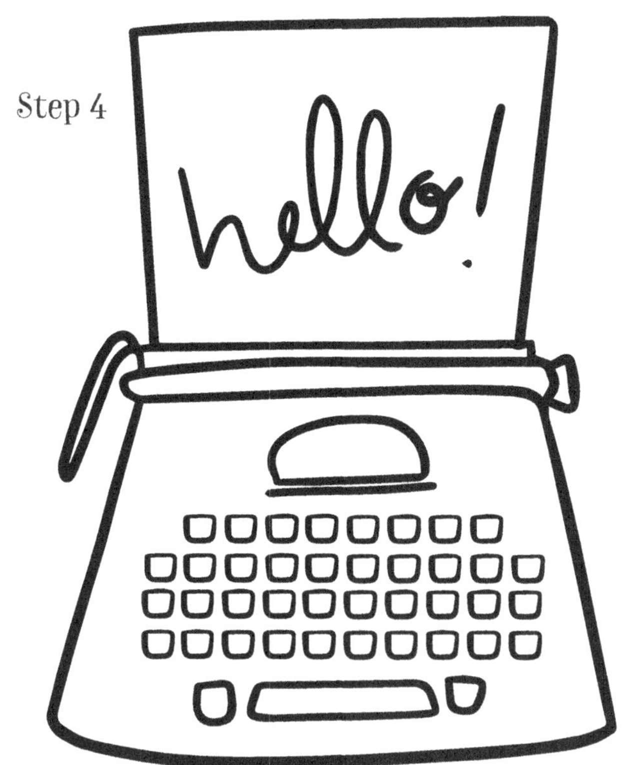

Draw your typewriter below:

Let's draw a

beehive

Step 1

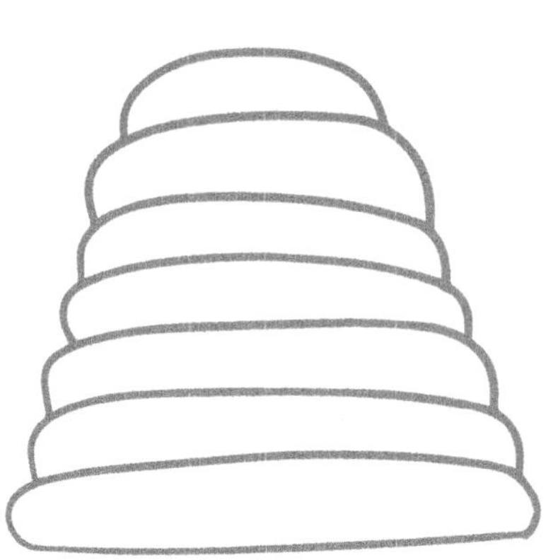

1. With a pencil draw ovals stacked on top of one another gradually getting smaller to form a beehive.

Step 2

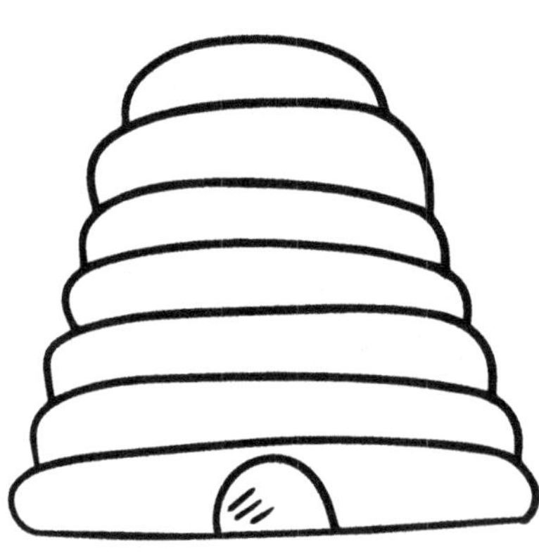

2. With a drawing pen trace over your pencil drawing. Add a little opening at the bottom of the hive.

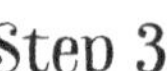

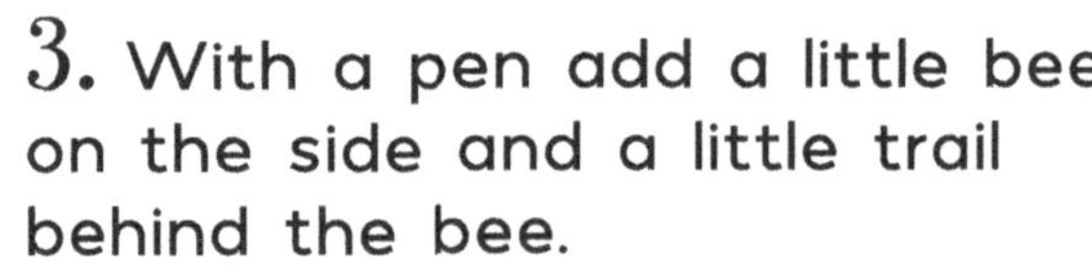

3. With a pen add a little bee on the side and a little trail behind the bee.

Step 3

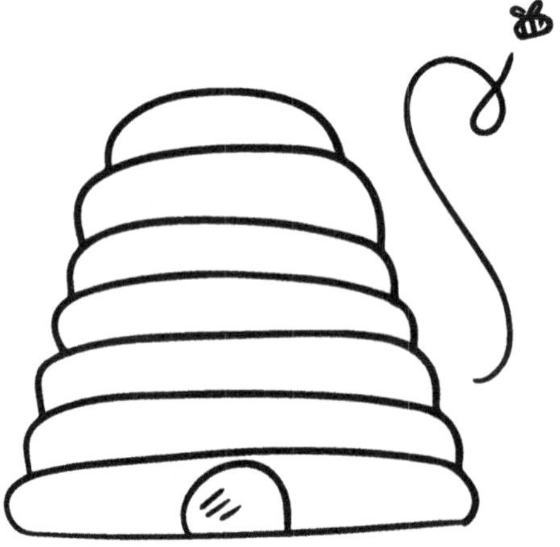

4. Finish the drawing by drawing flowers and leaves on each side of the beehive.

Step 4

Draw your beehive below:

Let's draw a butterfly

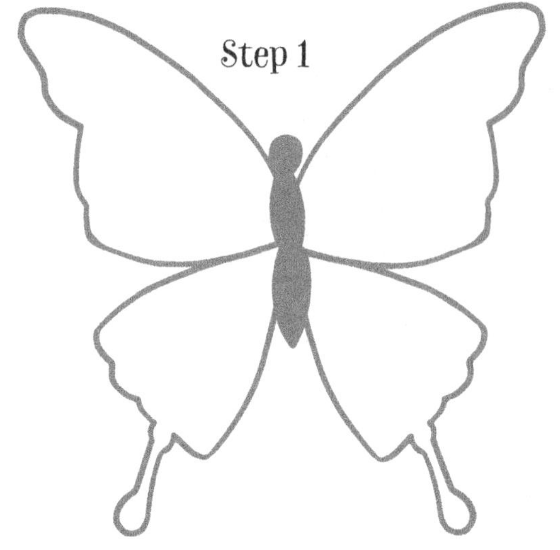

1. With a pencil draw the body of the butterfly. On each side sketch the wings making the fore wings (top) larger than the hind wings (bottom).

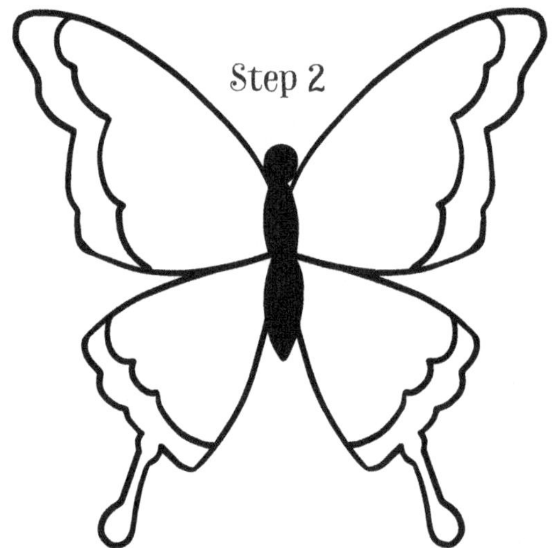

2. With a drawing pen trace over your pencil sketch. Add lines to form tips on the end of each butterfly wing.

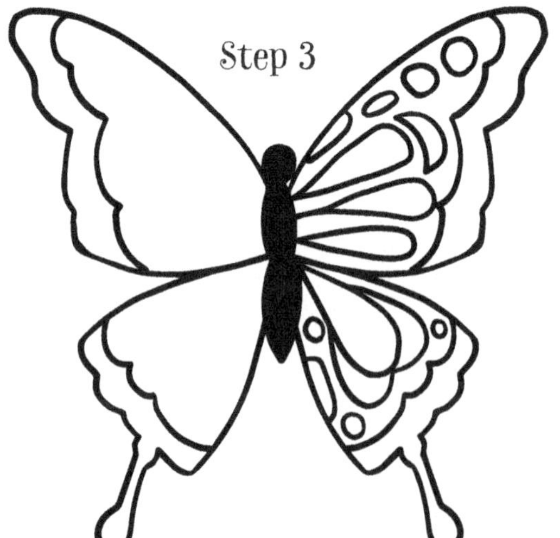

3. With a pen add circles, ovals, lines, and tear drop shapes into the inside of one side of the butterfly's wings.
Add as many details as you like.

4. Finish the butterfly by mirroring your drawings on the opposite wings with a pen.

Step 4

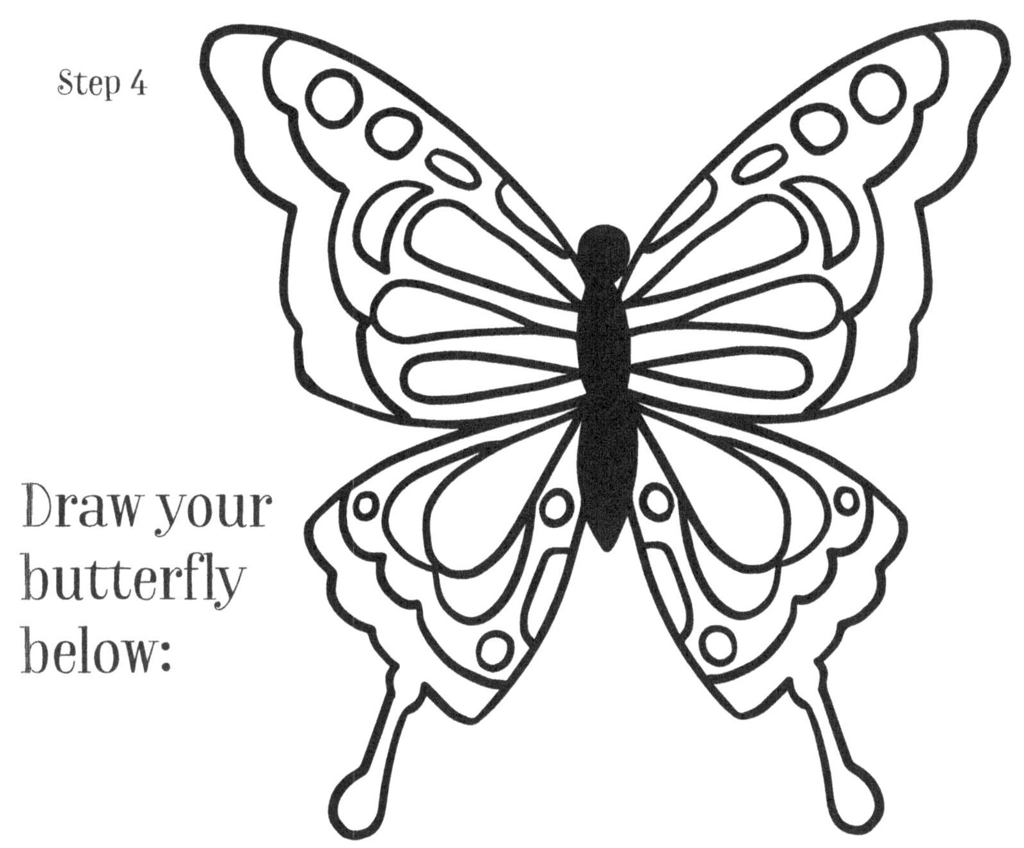

Draw your butterfly below:

Made in the USA
Coppell, TX
18 December 2021